The Reverse Effect

The 7 Life-Changing Principles

CLINTON M. MCCOY

The Reverse Effect: The 7 Life-Changing Principles
© 2015, 2016, 2018 by Clinton M. McCoy

Cover Design: Allison Arnett
Interior Design: Carol Earnest

Printed in the United States of America

ISBN-10-1540324176

ISBN-13-9781540324177

To order copies of this book, or to contact me for other coaching, visit me at:
www.reverseeffect.com or Amazon.com

Connect with me socially at:
Facebook: Clinton M McCoy
Instagram: Clinton M McCoy
LinkedIn: Clinton M McCoy
YouTube: Clinton M McCoy

TABLE OF CONTENTS

DEDICATIONS

I dedicate this book to God for loving me through my constant and continual mistakes, and for opening my eyes to the gifts of hope and purpose, not with the rods of fear and desperation. Thank You for gifting me with empowerment.

To my parents, Lionel McCoy and Betty Jo Ann Thompson, I acknowledge that without you, I would not be here today. You gave me the gift of life and a moral foundation during my early years. This foundation provided me with a reference point when I decided to get my life back on track.

A special dedication is reserved for my brother Carl McCoy. You have shown me the meaning of genuine forgiveness. Your strength and positive outlook on life have been an inspiration. Know that the twenty five years you have been incarcerated for a crime you did not commit were not in vain.

Additionally, to individuals who have decided their past will not dictate their future, I applaud you. Finally, to those of you who are finished interpreting your success through the lens of others' perspectives and have found the courage to pursue your dreams, welcome to the path less traveled.

ACKNOWLEDGMENTS

I want to thank my siblings Terry Griffin, Carl McCoy, Carlo McCoy, Sterling Rivers, and Valen McCoy. To my children, Kay Shara McCoy, Clinton McCoy, Jr., Dalante McCoy, Jecori Sala, Naa Shida McCoy, and Naazsir McCoy, you are my inspiration. All of these people had a significant influence on how and why I chose the material inside *The Reverse Effect*. They are major contributors to my drive to succeed.

To Dr. Joslyn A. Vann, thank you for your editing, proofreading and belief in my vision.

I HAVE A GIFT FOR YOU!

This planner will help you: **gain clarity**, and **become more productive in less than 30-days.**
Click the link below to claim your FREE copy:
bit.ly/thereverseeffectplanner

I am giving you this gift because I know what it has done for me and I cannot wait to see what it does for you. I thank you for taking this journey with me.

Clinton M. McCoy

INTRODUCTION

Have you found life to be confusing, stressful and unfulfilling? Do you feel like you have been dealt a lousy hand? Have you questioned how the experiences in your life fit together to create your purpose? Have you reached a point where you are ready for a change? If so, you have found the book that will reverse the results you have been getting out of life. You will learn the seven simple principles of manifestation that will help you create the life of your dreams.

I have made many mistakes in my life. Fortunately, I have learned many valuable lessons along the way. It is my mission to share the lessons I learned and inspire you to unlock the chains of your past and open the doors to your future.

"The Reverse Effect" is a program I built to help people transform their lives by turning the negatives into positives. The Seven Life-Changing Principles will change your life forever and ensure your success. I invite you to join me on a road of self-discovery, self-actualization and becoming an ultimate goal achiever. Your life without limits is just a few pages away.

The Reverse Effect is your comprehensive, step-by-step guide to success. Learn how to elevate yourself to a place of power and confidence. Develop the skills necessary to create the life of your dreams. When you combine a positive and proactive mindset with practical strategies for goal achievement, success is inevitable.

There is no secret to success, but there are specific keys that you will need to unlock the doors to your ultimate potential. For those new to the journey of personal development, understanding the principles and concepts can seem a little complicated.

Thus, one of the primary purposes of writing this book is to simplify these concepts and principles of success. I will use a layered and progressive approach that will help to establish a firm foundation of the ideas and techniques that successful people use every day to achieve success. I will share the tools I have used to create extraordinary changes in my life. I will also tell how I overcame some of my trials and tribulations. May this book bless you and encourage you to pursue your purpose, your dreams, and your passions.

It is time to transform your life!

Chapter 1

The Power of Principles

"Everyone has a purpose and an inner light that needs to shine."

The most important step we can take on this journey called life is a step towards discovering who you are and your reason for being. Everyone has a purpose and an inner light that needs to shine. When you find out your purpose, you will be on the path towards personal fulfillment. We all have a common goal in life, and that goal is to be happy!

I believe a life guided by principles is the key to personal fulfillment, overall success and true happiness. Principles are fundamental truths that serve as foundations for how we think, act, make decisions and attract positive people who align with the achievement of our purpose. They can be implemented over and over to help us become the master of our circumstances and transform our lives.

To be guided by principal means to function with clearly defined mindsets, actions, and ideals. Having a core set of principles is like possessing a consistent and reliable formula for success. Though the definition of success may vary from person to person, most successful people operate using principles that have contributed to their success.

We come by our principles in different ways. If we are wise (at least as adults), we gain them through our own experiences and reflections. Most of the time, we accept them from others, like our parents, religious institutions and unfortunately, for some, media programming. It is not always a bad thing to use others' principles, but adopting those principles without giving them much thought might leave you vulnerable to act in ways that are inconsistent with your personal goals and the nature of your being.

"The Reverse Effect" is my program, described in detail within the pages of this book, which will help you break the chains of your past and unlock the doors to your future. I will provide the tools needed to take back control of your life and manifest any reality you choose. This will require courage, open-mindedness, some self-forgiveness and several other life-changing principles which I will describe in this book.

The first step is summoning up the courage to think for yourself and be yourself, which is often easier said than done. Hold on, let me take that back because the true first step is figuring out who you are and not who you have been conditioned to be. The next step is to determine what you want to accomplish and why you want to achieve it. If you think for yourself and develop solid principles for success, you will undoubtedly make the most out of your life.

Being clear on your principles is important because they will affect aspects of your life, on multiple levels. This holds true for your relationships as well. For example, when you enter into relationships with other people, your principles and their principles will determine growth, stagnation or worse, toxicity. People who have similar ideologies and principles (i.e., those who are evenly yoked) are more productive. Those who do not have these similarities will suffer through constant misunderstandings and conflicts.

The great thing about creating and living by your own principles is they can be anything you want them to be. The only requirement is that they are authentic, meaning they must reflect your true nature and values. You will be faced with a lot of choices in life, and the decisions you make will reflect the principles you have. So, it won't be long before the people around you are able to tell the principles by which you are really operating. The worst thing you can be is a fraud, because the lies you tell yourself alter the truth that you live.

I have developed these seven life-changing principles over 20 years of making mistakes and spending a lot of time reflecting on them. I have learned that no matter how hard we try, we are going to make mistakes. Some of those mistakes are going to be extremely painful. Over time, I developed principles to help me prevent making the same mistakes over and over again. This way of learning and improving has helped me to develop a certain tenacity and resiliency to live life as the master of my circumstances.

I have learned that life is full of seemingly random and unexpected events, which ultimately connect us to our purpose (if we are paying attention). In this way, life is like a jigsaw puzzle, and our experiences are pieces of the puzzle. We gain a clear vision of our purpose through the process of organizing and connecting the events of our life. Once we understand how all these pieces have meaning and fit together, we become the master of our circumstances.

Each experience in life is essential. Through experiences, you acquire the knowledge, skills, and wisdom that it takes to become the best you. Life mastery comes through understanding and effectively applying what you have learned from your experiences. If you want to become a winner at life, you must first become the master of your life. Personal development and learning from your experiences will make you a champion.

A champion is one who continues to master his or her challenges until reaching their goals. If you want to succeed in life, you have to learn from your experiences. Remember that your goal is to be happy, be prosperous and live a life of abundance. Settle for nothing less! ***Tony Robbins***, motivational speaker and self-made millionaire, said: "I have come to believe that all my past failures and frustrations were laying the foundation for the understandings that have created the new level of living I now enjoy."

REFLECTIONS:

*Just like the 1980's "Hair Club for Men Commercials" ...
I am not just the creator of "The Reverse Effect" program,
I am also a member. In this book, I'm not going to talk about
abstract or theoretical applications for success. I will provide
practical and reliable strategies, tactics and processes to
ensure you will no longer be a victim of circumstances or
prisoner to your past. In the reflection sections of this book,
I will show how each of "The Seven Life-Changing
Principles" has helped me make incredible changes in my
own life. I will do that by telling some of my story.*

*When I was five years old, my friends and I were out walking
and came to a lagoon. One minute I was standing up, and
the next minute I felt myself being pushed into the water. At
the time, I did not know how to swim, and I began to sink. As
I descended further into the water, I remember thinking how
dark, murky, and cold it felt. It was an uneasy feeling.*

I can remember trying to hold my breath, but I was rapidly approaching the point when that would no longer be possible. I lost hope. I knew I was going to die. Then, in the midst of that hopeless situation, I saw a hand reaching down to me. The hand grabbed me by my wrists and pulled me toward the surface. As my head came up above the water, my lungs filled with air. Much relieved, I had a strong desire to thank the person who saved me. Looking all around, I found no one. I was completely alone...

"It was years later before the significance of this event became clear to me."

This event (which I have named "*The Lagoon*") was just one of the many pieces of my life's jigsaw puzzle. At the time, it had little meaning to me. But when I combined it with the bigger picture, it played a significant role in my spiritual growth and personal development. Understanding how this fits together with other pieces of my life's puzzle helped to shape my perspective and change my course.

I have reached the point in my life where I see no event or set of circumstances as meaningless. Learning from our experiences builds character and shapes us into who we are and will become. Even if we do not yet understand the purpose of an event and how it applies to our lives, every situation is relevant. Remember, nothing happens without reason, and everything has meaning, but only if you make it meaningful. We must pay attention if we want to take our lives in our desired direction.

On your journey of growth and self-actualization, you will experience hardships, setbacks, and triumphs. In the process of overcoming life's obstacles, you will gain the confidence required to become the master of your circumstances. To be the master of your circumstances is to be the master of your life. There is a saying, "The difference between progress and depression is often your purpose." Learn your purpose (or purposes), understand your *"Why,"* and there will be nothing to stop you from becoming the master of your circumstances.

Chapter 2

Positive Perspective

PRINCIPLE 1

Perspective is an attitude toward or way of regarding something; a point of view

In the next two chapters, I will talk about the impact of having a positive or negative perspective. Throughout this book, the words negative and positive are frequently used, but not from a moralistic standpoint or within the context of good or evil. Instead, it is about how they align with the achievement of your goals. I will draw from my personal experiences to illustrate how positive and negative perspectives can affect the decision-making process.

When negative friends, family, or viewpoints are mentioned, it is only within the context of the outcome you seek. It does not matter if the goal is attaining internal peace and happiness, becoming the successful CEO of a company, or making it as a professional athlete. Your viewpoint must align with the results that you desire. If it does not, it is toxic (negative) and will be an obstacle to your success.

Since I like to hear the good news first, I will start with the power of positive perspective. Having a positive outlook is the first of "The Seven Life-Changing Principles" for transforming your life. ***Perspective*** is a conscious interpretation of events and information.

The most valuable quality of perspective is that we can define it as we choose. One of the most abusive uses of perspective is the belief that everyone else's should match your own.

A fundamental principle of continued growth is broadening one's perspective; it is the key to limitless success. Learning to interpret your viewpoint positively is often the key to success or failure in life. Maintaining a positive outlook has had a remarkable impact on creating positive change in my life today. I know this way of viewing life circumstances will help you transform your life as well.

As it is par for the course (of life), there are going to be situations that we cannot control. There are times in our lives when it seems that everything goes right: we're in the zone. Then there are times when it seems as if nothing goes our way no matter how hard we try. However, we can manage how we view even the most challenging times. We can manage our perspective.

Your thoughts govern the choices you make and actions you take in life. If your thoughts are negative, you have a higher likelihood of making decisions which produce negative results. On the other hand, maintaining a positive perspective is a shield against the crushing weight of disappointment and failure. It is the shining light when it seems you are surrounded by the darkness of despair, and it will help you keep sight of the bigger picture.

REFLECTIONS:

Six years ago, I woke up to find that all of my Landscaping equipment was stolen. In an instant, $16,000 worth of business equipment had vanished! I remember this just as if it were yesterday. Coming back from a morning walk, my children's grandmother (visiting from New Jersey) noticed *that my equipment wasn't in the yard. She knocked on my bedroom door to ask where I had stored the equipment. Realizing what she said, I quickly ran to the windows and looked out. Sure enough, it was gone.*

I quickly closed the blinds only to peer out again, hoping that the equipment would magically reappear. The parking area where I had left it was now an empty spot. At that moment, all I could do was shake my head. I had worked hard over a period of three years to build the business. As the gravity of what happened began to sink in, I felt broken.

As I processed my current situation and the potential consequences of this event, I began to change my way of thinking. I realized I could have lost more than material things. The situation could have been much worse. I could have lost this equipment in a traffic accident injuring myself and others. I realized if I was going to make it through what just happened, I had to maintain a positive perspective. I focused my attention on my knowledge, skill set, and support. Equally as important, I had to concentrate on my next steps. I knew the road ahead of me was going to be difficult, and I was ready to meet that challenge. This shift in my mindset brought about a sense of clarity.

As I think back to that day, I remember that my girlfriend was far more upset than me. I just did not see how harmful thoughts would fix the problem. I refused to be defeated. I could not fathom the idea of being down and depressed while the people who stole my equipment might be somewhere happy and profiting. There was no way I was going back to the street life. I simply refused!

"Stop making excuses and put forth the effort to get to where you want to go."

Having a positive perspective will always keep you moving forward, but it will not shield you from setbacks. The positive manner in which I interpreted my situation aided me in recovering from what could have had a cataclysmic impact on my livelihood. I have learned that having a positive perspective will not solve all your problems, but it is a good start.

Overcoming obstacles and achieving your goals always requires action. Rarely do great things in life come easy. Taking action and having a positive perspective will increase the odds of your success. One of the main things that hold people back from achievement is excuses.

Once you stop making excuses and began putting forth the effort to get to where you want to go, everything becomes possible. If you want success in your life and if you're going to overcome obstacles, your perspective has to change. I have learned that the only thing that you must do to accomplish your dreams is to remove "like" and "easy" as essential variables from your equation for success.

There are a lot of variables involved in becoming successful. Having a positive perspective will be one of your most valuable tools. It will allow you to remain focused on the bigger picture instead of being dragged down by individual negative circumstances of everyday life. This reminds me of a story my grandfather once told me:

REFLECTIONS:

> *"There was an old man who lived on a farm with his son, and they had one horse to help them to till the ground. One morning a storm blew the fence down, and the horse ran off. All the villagers came to the old man and said, "Wow! What bad luck you're having." The old man replied nothing. Then,*

three days later the horse came back with three mares in tow. The villagers were overjoyed as they replied, "Wow! You are having such good luck!" The old man replied nothing.

A couple of weeks later, while riding the wild mare, the son fell off the horse and broke his leg in two places. Once again, the villagers commented on the old man's turn of bad luck, and yet he said nothing.

Weeks went by, and the Army generals came to the town to sign up all non-disabled men and young boys to go off and fight in the war; however, they could not take the old man's son because of his injury."

When going through the trials and tribulations of life, it is often difficult to stay positive and to stay focused on the bigger picture. Like any other skill, it requires practice to maintain a positive perspective. So, when tough times come around, look at them as an opportunity to become stronger. When you are met with adversity just remember the saying, *"What doesn't kill you only makes you stronger."*

PERSPECTIVE:

Please do not wish me luck. Wishing me luck means that you do not believe I am prepared to accomplish my goals. "Perspective"[100]

"Perspective"[100] = This reference denotes I am giving My Perspective 100%

Chapter 3

Negative Perspective

"Positive perspectives and negative perspectives are equally sharp edges of the same sword."

The manner in which we process information and events around us has a direct impact on the actions we take; your perspective is powerful. Positive and negative perspectives are opposite edges of the same sword. The creative power of a negative outlook is just as dominant as that of a positive perspective. If we believe that every storm cloud has a silver lining, we will always have a sense of hope. However, if we see every storm cloud as a portent of doom, we will live in perpetual despair.

We interpret events around us through our feelings, thoughts, and belief systems. It is through these interpretations that we make all of our decisions. Having a negative or positive perspective is the deciding factor in determining whether we progress or become stagnant. In a sense, we see people or things not for who or what they are, but for how and what we believe them to be.

For example, let's say that there is a cup of water on the table next to a trash can. Two men walk in and look at the cup of water, but from different perspectives. One just came in from working in the hot sun, but the other hates water. Do you think they will view the cup in the same manner? Probably not! To one, the container near the trash can may appear as a terrible disappointment, but to the other, it's a welcome refreshment after a hard day's work in the sun. No matter their feelings about the cup of water on the table, it still will not change the fact that it's just a cup of water.

Here is an example of how my negative perspective affected me for a period:

REFLECTIONS:

Like most teenagers, at the age of 15, I thought I was smarter than my parents. I thought the rules and regulations my father wanted me to follow while in his household were strict and irrational. I thought I knew what was best for me. I thought I was ready to be grown.

Thinking I was ready to take on the world, I left my father's home and went to live with my mother in South Florida. Going from a military environment to living in the hood was a polar shift. While living with my dad, I thought that drugs like alcohol and marijuana were hard drugs. However, it was nothing compared to what I encountered within the first three weeks of living in South Florida.

I had no idea what the streets were really like. Drugs like crack, cocaine, and heroin were everywhere, and so were junkies. It wasn't long after arriving in South Florida that the relationship with my mom became rocky. I decided that I no longer wanted to live by anyone's rules and regulations. Thinking that I could make it on my own, I turned to the streets. That turned out to be one of the many bad decisions I would make over the next 12 years of my life.

The Reverse Effect

Let me give you some background on how I ended up going to live with my mom. About six months before I left my dad, I had my first encounter with the law. I was arrested for aggravated assault. The charges were dropped because of my dad's military status, but I did end up spending a week in juvenile detention.

While there, I met a guy who always talked about the "Crips" which is a gang. I found this to be very fascinating. This was at a time when gangsta rap was coming into popularity, and it seemed like a cool thing to do. At the time, I was 14 years old with no self-identity and low self- esteem. I decided I wanted to be in a gang.

When I got out of the juvenile detention facility, I decided that this was going to be how I identified myself—as the ultimate "Crip." To me, being in a gang represented being part of a family and having respect and self-identity. That is the identity I brought with me when I decided to live with my mother. Thinking I was smart and ready for the world, I left my mom's house and turned to the streets. It wasn't too long afterward that I realized I was neither of those things.

Nevertheless, I had too much pride to ask my mom or dad for help. It wasn't long before I started to realize that the streets were far more difficult than I had imagined. Soon, I found myself being manipulated and taken advantage of... I felt betrayed... my trust was abused. After about three months, I became a heavy drinker, started using cocaine, and tried crack cocaine. Using drugs was my way of coping with the harsh realities of living in the streets.

At 15 years of age, life on the streets was tough. I felt I had to resort to criminal activity to survive. I was homeless. I sold drugs for food and shelter. On good days I would rent motel rooms. And on not so good nights, I would stay in hallways or a park. Slowly but surely, I started to become callous. As a result, I only saw the worst in people, and this ultimately led to my breaking point.

About 3 o'clock one rainy morning, I was coming down from a cocaine high while sitting in an abandoned hallway. I could not afford to rent a motel room because I had spent my money on cocaine. I was feeling sorry for myself and was contemplating suicide. I thought about all the times I had allowed myself to be a victim and the times when someone had made me a victim.

Memories of sexual and physical abuse resurfaced. I felt that the people in whom I had put my trust and the God in whom I had put my faith had betrayed me. So, as I stepped from the hallway with rain and tears running down my face, I screamed out, "NO MORE!"

As I stood in the rain, I thought about a 1993 movie I once saw, "A Bronx Tale." The gangster, Sonny, was asked, "What would you rather be, loved or feared?" He replied, "It's nice to be both, but very difficult." He went on to explain that fear lasts longer than love because it is fear that promotes loyalty. He explained how power and money could instill fear in others and allow you to take control.

It was at this time that I let out one last desperate cry to God. I said, "If you are all-knowing and if you are real, then you have to know that I have to see to believe. And, at this point in my life, I don't see enough to believe." I waited for what seemed to be an eternity for an answer. None came. I thought, "OK! That's fine!" I decided that I had no time or

*room in my life for a God. From that point on over the next
14 years, I was an atheist.*

Viewing reality through the filters of pain, hate, and negativity will
only lead to more of the same. For example, if you run roses through
a filter of garbage they will still be roses, but they will smell like
garbage. It is the same as filtering life through a negative perspective.

My negative perspective cost me so much in opportunity,
relationships, and growth. It took me years to realize that my
negative perspective was creating my negative reality. The very fact
that I thought so little of myself, and my life, was the reason I was
receiving so little. I, like many others, underestimated the power of
perspective.

It was years later before I realized the impact that negative decisions
had on my life and the people around me. I wholeheartedly embraced
the belief that I would not live past 27 years of age. So, I decided I
was going to live and die like a gangster.

As stated earlier, positive and negative perspectives are equally
sharp edges of the same sword. However, a positive outlook
allows you to cut through the darkness of pain, setbacks, and the
sometimes overbearing weight of circumstances. Though a negative
perspective can also cut through obstacles, rarely does it do so
without simultaneously cutting a piece of you. Understanding the
power of your viewpoint is vital to overcoming barriers and creating
change in your life, and achieving all your goals.

PERSPECTIVE:

Your success should be measured against the fulfillment of your potential, not against someone else's accomplishments.
"Perspective"[100]

Chapter 4

Mastering Your Mindset

PRINCIPLE 2

Developing effective mindsets for goal achievement

The vast majority of your actions are fueled by your thoughts, perspectives, and mindset. It stands to reason that a change in your perspective and mindset will affect a difference in your efforts. Your actions are typically reflections of your thoughts, feelings, and priorities. Most of your actions are prompted by your mindset (or combination of mindsets) which justifies a particular behavior or response to a set of circumstances.

Your perspective is your overall view of how you interpret the world around you. It is the big picture. Perspectives contain both intellectual and emotional elements that affect your perceptions and actions. They guide what you think, how you feel, and how you react to people and circumstances. The way you interpret the world around you is formed by a combination of values, beliefs, preferences, and attitudes.

Underneath the umbrella of your perspective, you have your mindset. The mindset is the driving component that supports your perspective. It is the force that either drives you forward, takes you in reverse, or keeps you going around in circles. When you combine a positive perspective with the right mindset, anything becomes possible.

I describe your perspective as being the coach of a football team. The coaches have the overall vision of how they believe the team can win each game. It is up to the coach (perspective) to implement different tactics (mindsets) to accomplish the goal of winning the game (goal achievement).

They have tactics (mindsets) such as choosing to operate the offense in a way that will help them achieve the goal of scoring touchdowns (goals). Will they implement a balanced running and passing, or will they choose to run the football more as a strategy to win?

In keeping with the bigger picture, the coach has an overall plan (perspective) on how to prevent the other team from scoring points. An essential component to the goal of winning the game involves having a strong defense (mindset) as well as a strong offense (mentality). How the coach views offense and defense will determine which tactics are chosen.

You may ask, "How will this perspective and mindset help transform me into a purposefully driven goal achieving machine?" Mindsets are beliefs and fundamental qualities about yourself that fuel your actions. There are many types of mindsets, but for purposes of goal achievement and personal development, I will focus on four categories.

The first two categories of mindsets are ***Reactive and Proactive***. Remember, it is our mindset that supports how we interpret the world around us. What does it mean to be reactive, as opposed to proactive? The word "reactive" means you are acting in response to a situation rather than creating or controlling it. You are allowing people and situations to manage your choices because you are not ahead of the game. Or, you are just going with the flow of things instead of taking charge and directing the flow your way.

When you have a reactive mindset, life's ups and downs will consistently catch you off-guard. With a reactive mindset, you are always on the defensive, only dodging life's punches. It is difficult to make progress when you are continually fending off the blows of life. In this defensive mentality, you rarely get a chance to throw any punches back at life.

By contrast, a proactive mindset creates opportunities to solve problems before they become a significant issue. Using the previous boxing analogy, instead of dodging and taking life's punches, you can now go on the offensive. Being proactive means anticipating upcoming events and using foresight to deal with potential problems. The table below summarizes the fundamental differences between proactive and reactive mindsets.

Proactive and Reactive Mindsets

Proactive Mindset	Reactive Mindset
Solve matters before they get out of hand	Caught off guard by life's circumstances
Study, think, and plan ahead to defend challenges	Continually dodging life's punches with little ability to defend
Flexible and adapt well to change	Resist change and ignore danger

Look at life as your opponent, and circumstances as potential obstacles in your way. By studying your opponent (life), you are now able to see patterns in events (circumstances). Through experience, you sharpen your ability to predict where the punches (ups and downs) are coming from. Over time, this provides you with the knowledge to either punch, bob or weave. People with a proactive mindset have a significant advantage over most circumstances in life. They are flexible and adapt well to changes.

On the other hand, people with a reactive mindset tend to resist change until the last possible second, often losing the advantage of choice. The reactive mindset person ignores the danger signs and the red flags of life. Consequently, this invites serious problems where the molehills of life become hard-to-pass mountains. The proactive mindset allows you to stay a few steps ahead of the game. Rather than waiting for circumstances to dictate your actions, it gives you the opportunity to change long before the risk becomes too severe.

Two more mindset categories are ***Positive*** and ***Negative***. I will align these with fixed and growth mindsets as in Carol Dweck's *Mindset: The Psychology of Success*. The negative mindset is comparable to what she calls a fixed mindset, and the positive mindset is a growth mindset. A fixed mindset assumes that our personality, intelligence, and creative ability can't change in any meaningful way. This mindset is stuck in a fixed position negating any opportunity for growth.

People with a fixed mindset believe you either are or aren't good at something based on your inherent nature; it's just who you are. A fixed mindset is the enemy of change and progress. Conversely, you can have what she calls a ***growth mindset*** which thrives on challenge and sees failure as an opportunity for growth and stretching our existing abilities. The table below summarizes the differences between the fixed and growth mindsets.

Fixed and Growth Mindset

Fixed Mindset	Growth Mindset
You want to hide your flaws, so you're not judged or labeled a failure.	Your flaws are just a to-do list of things to improve.
You stick with what you know to keep up your confidence.	You keep up your confidence by always pushing into the unfamiliar to make sure you're always learning.
You look inside yourself to find your real passion and purpose as if this is a hidden thing.	You commit to mastering valuable skills regardless of mood. You know passion and purpose come from doing great work, which comes from expertise and experience.
Failures define you.	Failures are temporary setbacks.

From these mindsets spring a lot of our behavioral patterns, relationships, success (in both professional and personal contexts), and ultimately our capacity for happiness. Taking control and reshaping your perspective empowers you to interpret life events and situations in a manner that pushes you toward the completion of your goals.

Instead of taking the loss of a job as a failure, you adopt a proactive, growth mindset that allows you to interpret it as an opportunity to learn. You actively start looking for a better job and focus on developing your skills set. For some, it can be an opportunity to grow that entrepreneurial spirit and be on the path to becoming *"Application Independent,"* a phrase I've coined.

Thirteen years after passing my GED, I decided it was time to go back to school. First, I had to take the college placement tests to see which courses I could take. I did not score that high, so my first semester of college consisted of prerequisite courses. I did rather well in the beginning, but the lack of proper study habits soon changed that. I realized that I was not prepared to be a successful student, so I started failing.

I recognized the fact that I was at least ten years older than my classmates, and this started to bother me. I had a negative mindset, and it was not helping me progress. It was a full year of failing classes before I finally had enough. I said to myself, "If a million other people can pass these classes, there is no way that I cannot do the same."

This was when the second life-changing principle helped me to transform my life. Using a growth mindset, I started looking at my failures as opportunities to learn and not as a reflection of any inherent inability. I began using all the resources at my disposal to help me achieve my goal of getting good grades. This meant joining study groups, tutoring, and learning different learning techniques (visual, auditory, tactile/ kinesthetic).

Being proactive put me in a position to prepare and be ready for the questions on the upcoming tests. Networking with other students allowed me to choose teachers who were more suited to my particular learning styles. Utilizing one-on-one tutoring allowed me to get my questions answered in a comfortable setting. I went on to graduate from the Florida College of Jacksonville with an AA degree.

From this experience, I learned that growth is not always predicated on your current level of ability. More so, it's about the way you look at things based on the mindsets you have adopted. Having a positive and growth mindset will help you overcome many obstacles in life. Conversely, having a fixed and negative mindset will stop you in your tracks. If you want things to change in your life, you have to be willing to take a close look at the mindsets you choose.

Dr. Wayne Dyer, a self-made millionaire, author, and motivational speaker, said, *"Change the way you look at things, and the things you look at will change."* Taking control of your future and achieving success in life depends on your view of yourself and the world around you. The decisions you this make in life are governed by the combination of perspective and mindset. Staying positive and focusing on your growth instead of your failures will help you overcome all of life's obstacles.

You master your mindset by learning how to change the way you look at things. This is a powerful skill anyone can learn. How we choose to view a situation is precisely the way it is, and it does not matter how anyone else sees it. So, if you decide to view a situation positively, it will always have a positive effect on you.

"You will experience opposition and disappointments, but you will always have the power of choice to guide your outcome."

Does this mean that life is going to be a bed of roses, or that every day is a sunny day? No, it does not. You will experience opposition and disappointments, but you will always have the power of choice to guide your outcome. You can choose to be positive and learn from the experiences or have a negative perspective and be disappointed by life when you don't get the results you desire.

When you apply Principles #1 and #2 to transforming your life, everything becomes possible. Adopt a positive perspective and support it with the right mindsets, and watch how you achieve your goals.

PERSPECTIVE:

Your success should be measured against the fulfillment of your potential, not against someone else's accomplishments. "Perspective"[100]

Chapter 5

Taking Action Against the Past

Our past can be our most potent enemy or our greatest ally. Even though our past is a part of us, our history does not have to define who we are in the present or define our future. We all have experiences that we would like to forget, forgive, or seek forgiveness for in some way. The only way wounds from our past can continue to fester and grow is when there is an unwillingness to let the past go.

As I look back over my life, the sexual and physical abuse I endured as a child fueled a lot of my rage and self-destructive behavior. Subconsciously, the past governed my decision-making processes. I had years of self-destructive behavior before I realized my past was controlling me. Though my history was only memories, I allowed it to have power and control over my life.

> *"I have learned that I gain nothing positive from holding on to a negative past."*

The past, while real at one time, is only a concept or series of thoughts that I give power. Those thoughts became my constant reality - a reality that I had to change. I have learned that I gain nothing positive form holding on to a negative thought. Remember, negativity doesn't have to cause pain and strife; it is simply anything that does not align with the achievement of your current goals. For most of us, learning to forgive and letting go of our past is tough. Nonetheless, it is something that we can achieve using the power of our minds. For most of us, one of the things that makes taking control of our past so difficult is that we have allowed our history to become more than memories. We have allowed those memories to take form and grow into separate entities. In some cases, our past even talks to us. It has a voice and distinct personality.

Have you ever been in a situation where you met someone who seemed to be kind and genuinely interested in you? Have you ever found your former self having a conversation with your current self about a past life event? Your current self might say, "Wow! I'm really interested in that person, and they seem to like me. I think I want to open up and give them a chance." However, your past self or negative memory tells you, "Do not let them in. They're not good for you. They only want to hurt you like so-and-so."

A lot of us have found ourselves in this exact situation. And most of the time, our negative past ruins our future happiness. The longer we allow negative memories to rule our lives, the harder it is to get rid of them. There comes a time in life when we want to heal ourselves and grow. To evolve through self-healing, we have to be able to take action against the harmful memories from our past, to let them go.

The most important quality to becoming successful, overcoming obstacles, and obtaining amazing personal growth is to change the way we think. We all possess the power to create positive change in our lives. Everything starts with the way we process what we know. We should always utilize the knowledge we have acquired, including negative memories, to become the best version of ourselves.

There is a quote from *The Unity of Knowledge and Action* by Wang Yang Ming, a 15th century Chinese Neo-Confucian philosopher, that says, "If you don't apply the knowledge you know, then that knowledge is useless." This means knowing, and the useful application of that knowledge, are two entirely different things. With that, I believe that understanding our past and learning from it are not the same.

Here's an example of knowing something but not applying that knowledge. Let's say your goal is to get in shape. You possess the knowledge of hundreds of different exercises, but if you never apply this knowledge, did the possession of that knowledge have any value? I say the answer is an emphatic, "No!"

Zhu Xi, a 12th century Song Dynasty scholar, states: "The mind, the agent by which man rules his body, it is one and not divided. It is a subject and not objects. It controls the external world. It is not a slave to it." I interpret this to mean that all the tools we need to change and heal ourselves are already within ourselves. Of course, there are outside things that can help you sharpen these tools, but the tools are inside of you.

I often see people using external remedies in attempts to heal internal wounds. I compare this to trying to stop a leaking dam with a couple of Band-Aids. These problems often persist because we allow them to. For years, I used drugs and alcohol to mask the painful memories of my childhood. It was not until I accepted that my past was in the past that I was able to create a future that I desired.

PERSPECTIVE:

Let go of your past dreams and failures so you can focus on creating your best future. Remember the future you want is not owed to you—it must be created. "Perspective"[100]

Chapter 6

Self-Forgiveness

PRINCIPLE 3

Self-forgiveness is the condition in the mind that allows the full flow of Life Energy and personal potential.

Forgiveness is a powerful, life-changing principle—a tool for growth that is necessary for healing. It is vital to becoming the strongest and best version of yourself. Unfortunately, most people believe forgiveness is something that starts with other people. I say this because requiring closure from a source outside of yourself is essentially giving up your power. If you want closure, then close that door and move on. While forgiving others is essential, forgiving ourselves is equally, if not more, important.

Real forgiveness starts from within, and harnessing this ability is crucial to your life journey. Most of the demons and mountains that stand in the way of our success are of our own creation. True forgiveness is a process that happens over time; it is not instantaneous. There must be an in-depth and honest inventory of one's self before a life-changing journey can have any reasonable expectation of success.

As with any long journey, you do not want to carry excess and useless baggage. Make no mistake about it, the journey of personal transformation is a long road full of ups and downs. Learning how to rid yourself of that excess baggage, as soon as possible, will make the journey a lot easier down the road. I often tell people, "Do not waste time and energy trying to forgive others or searching for someone else to give you closure."

"Real forgiveness starts from within, and harnessing this ability is a valuable tool."

To begin the process of self-forgiveness, you must first forgive yourself for past mistakes. The next step is to remember that memories are only that—MEMORIES. Do not give them power. These two factors were challenging for me, particularly when those memories involved hurting the people I cared for. I will admit that there are some memories that you will not be able to forgive yourself for completely. Nevertheless, you have to put those memories in proper perspective and take away their power.

One such memory is the knowledge that I was involved in actions that resulted in my brother getting sentenced to 27 years in a Florida State Penitentiary. Knowing that my closest loved one is currently serving year 22 of his sentence for something he was not a part of is very painful. Though this negative memory plagues me, I continue to use it to motivate me to do better. I made a vow that when my brother is released, I will make sure that he is "Application Independent."

*"**Application Independent**" is a term I coined to say that I will no longer require outside sources for a job or approval. I will do everything within my power to make sure he will not have to fill out any applications for income or social acceptance.*

In my experience, I've learned that it is more effective to deal with one negative memory at a time. It is next to impossible to forgive yourself for all wrong decisions in one instance. Remember, negative memories are thoughts we give power, and we can take that control away.

"Focused energy is stronger..."

Therefore, as the saying goes, "See the forest, but attack one tree at a time." The fact is, focused energy is much stronger then scattered energy. So, you must deal with one thing at a time. And before you know it, you will become the master of your past and controller of your future.

PERSPECTIVE:

We are the only reason others have power over us. "Perspective"[100]

Chapter 7

Self-Acceptance

PRINCIPLE 4

*Self-Acceptance is an individual's satisfaction
or happiness with oneself.*

Self-Acceptance is the fourth life-changing principle, and sometimes it can be the hardest. Learning to accept ourselves for who we are is often easier said than done. Since birth, we have been bombarded with people telling us how we should think, act and believe. Undoing that conditioning is strenuous. Personal growth is a lifelong learning process that requires constant change, effort, and courage. Since we are ever-changing, accepting ourselves for who we are is a journey without a finish line.

Accepting yourself for who you are first requires learning who you are. Acceptance is a verb, so only speaking the words will not cut it. We all have said the words, "I am happy with who I am," never really understanding who we are. This does not create change. Instead, it's more of a shift in mental perspective, and shifting perspective is key to unlocking the doors to your happiness.

A shift in your mental perspective will empower you to seek progress and self-fulfillment; to never settle for less than what you are capable of or to use other people's success or failures as your yardstick.

Most self-improvement books will try to sell you on things such as putting a thought out into the universe and allowing it to manifest itself into a reality. People from different schools of religious thought place emphasis on prayer as a catalyst for change in your life. By contrast, although these things may work for those who ascribe to them, I believe that we should focus on action as the primary tool for long-lasting and meaningful life-changing results. Now, I am not devaluing the power of prayer, but I think that prayer without action is less effective.

"Faith without works is dead."

When I talk about action, I'm not talking about pointless movement. What I am referring to is an effective action which will allow you to proceed in a direction that you want to go with the least amount of resistance.

Note that when I say self-acceptance, I am not talking about the commonly held point of view.

"This is just the way that I am." Most people do not admit who they are to themselves. Instead, they take a stagnant viewpoint of themselves. They are ultimately paralyzing any potential for change that they might have.

There are millions of people who aren't willing to look at their current situation and accept the truth of it. For example, using a scale of 1 to 10 as a way to measure personal success within someone's life, many people who have the potential to be a ten will max out at 5.

The Reverse Effect

I compare self-acceptance to those maps that you see at rest stop areas that say, "You are here." Establishing exactly where you are in life provides the perfect starting point for you to proceed efficiently in any direction you may want to go. In most cases, it takes a defining moment in someone's life to give them the power to take that hard look at themselves.

REFLECTIONS:

Another defining moment in my life happened when I was 26 years old. I was playing a game called "Run the stop signs." We would find a street with multiple stop signs, or stoplights, race all the way to the end without stopping; turn around and come back. On this particular day, I was motorcycle racing with myself just for the fun of it. It was only me challenging life.

As I ran one stop sign and two intersection lights, I was thinking to myself, "Wow, you are on top of the world." Speeding through the fourth stop sign, I felt unstoppable. My declaration at that moment was, "I don't need anyone or anything. No gods, no family, and no friends. I am a gangster!"

A nice-looking lady was walking by. I pulled over for about two seconds and patted her on the butt. Then I looked up to see that I had a short stretch before the next stop sign. To show off, I popped the clutch. Accelerating toward the stop sign, I heard a voice in my head say, "Clint, you had better stop at the next stop sign." It's funny because, at that time in my life, I had been an atheist for about ten years. I verbally replied, "F*#k that S#*t. I don't give a F*#k!"

Then, as I put my head down and gave it more gas, a car pulled out about 15 yards in front of me. At 40 miles per hour, 15 yards evaporated in two long seconds. Without enough time to alter my fate, I conceded to the consequences of my actions and braced myself for the worst.

Slamming into the back of the car, the force of the impact sent me soaring through the air for about 15 feet—so I was told. It took me about 30 seconds to re-orient myself after I hit the ground. I remember thinking to myself, "Wow, I survived." I was elated to be still alive, and for a brief moment, I felt invincible. However, after a quick self-diagnosis, I realized that I was severely injured.

After the adrenaline rush wore off, I started feeling more physical pain than I had ever felt in my life. I lay there on the hot summer South Florida asphalt for almost an hour before I was taken to the hospital. It wasn't the agony that I felt then, but the events that happened within that hour which would be the catalyst for me becoming the person I am today.

For two weeks, I was hospitalized with multiple breaks in the tibia and fibula regions of my leg; my elbow was busted up, and I had road burns everywhere. Worse than all of that was the realization that I was now entirely dependent on other people's kindness. I even needed assistance to use the bathroom.

Where I used to pride myself on my independence, now I found myself asking for assistance with the simplest tasks. This brought back my childhood memories of abuse. For the first time in years, I had to deal with the fear of vulnerability. I knew it was time for me to start looking back over the past years of my life and questioning, "Do I love myself? Am I living to be the person that I want to be, or am I just running from myself and hiding from the past?"

To learn to accept yourself, you first have to be aware of how to forgive yourself. Think about the parts of yourself that you wish to change because you think it will make people like you.

Those of us who have the fortune to look back over our lives in retrospect should never witness a day without appreciation. The ability to forgive ourselves and others is a priceless gift. This gift represents the birth of new opportunities to grow and move forward in life.

Self-acceptance is a powerful practice that allows the ego to be altered. Learning to accept yourself for who you are is the starting point for real self-love. You set an unshakable standard that will undoubtedly elevate you to receive what you desire and deserve.

The 6th century philosopher Lao Tzu said in the *Tao Te Ching*, "Care about people's approval, and you will be their prisoner." This does not mean to walk around with your nose in the air oblivious to what people think about you. Do not let what other people think about you distort your view of yourself.

Do not allow someone else's standard or viewpoint on love, success, and happiness shape and mold what will bring you love, prosperity, and happiness. Other people's beliefs about you are projections of their internal world, and they may or may not have a shred of truth about you as a person.

I believe that we become what we think about. If you constantly think about what other people think of you, you will inevitably become who those people think you are. From birth, we are taught to conform and meet someone else's expectations of us. It's time to discover what makes us strong and unique (our purpose) and to pursue goals that give our lives **meaning.**

Dr. Abraham Maslow, the famed humanistic psychologist, said, *"What is necessary to change a person is to change his awareness of himself."* When we accept ourselves for who we are, every route toward self-improvement becomes shorter.

PERSPECTIVE:

Sticks and stones may break my bones, but looking into myself sometimes hurts worse. "Perspective"[100]

Chapter 8

Thirteen Seconds

Life is full of ups and downs and lessons to be learned. Unfortunately, most of us go through life in a reactive mindset; settling for just going with the flow of life and rolling with the punches. In my earlier years, I was no exception. However, my lights were eventually turned on. I had a spiritual awakening.

In this chapter, I will give you detailed accounts leading up to that defining moment or epiphany. I didn't know it at the time, but that would be the beginning of the end of some of the darkest times in my life. While having one of my closest dances with death, I heard the tune of a purpose-driven life.

"I remembered flying through the air and thinking
I was not going to survive this."

My motorcycle accident resulted in a two-week stay in the hospital. I took the opportunity to reflect on the unbelievable revelation and choices presented to me. The events of that hour constantly replayed in my mind. I remember flying through the air and thinking I was not going to survive.

When I hit the ground, I flipped and tumbled at least 15 feet before coming to a stop. As I said previously, I felt invincible. I recalled saying to myself, "I am a f*#king warrior, and nothing can stop me." I then remember thinking, "I'm going to get up and walk over to the shade because this hot a#$ ground is killing me." I also remember laughing to myself as I saw the bones sticking out of my leg. I thought, "Well, that shade option is now off the table." To this day, I have no idea why I thought that was funny.

As a crowd started to gather around, I became determined not to allow anyone to see me in pain. After about five minutes, the initial adrenaline rush started to wear off and the pain from my injuries rapidly increased. Moments later, the pain of my protruding shin-bone started to become unbearable.

It would be another 10 minutes before the ambulance would arrive, but even then, they would be of no help to me. A call from the local authorities came over the radio telling the paramedics not to touch me until the police arrived. They said I was to be considered armed and dangerous and not to be approached.

REFLECTIONS:

By this time in my life, I was considered a menace to society. I'd been incarcerated numerous times and was a drug-dealing gang member. I'd been to trial by judge and jury four times, and had no respect for people or the law. With this perspective, it is not difficult to see why the first responders did not override the call over the radio. The only person helping me was a stranger who had placed my head in his lap so that the ground wouldn't burn my face.

Though I was only on the ground for 30 minutes, it seemed like an eternity. It was at this point that the pain was too much. No longer was I the warrior and no longer did I care about the people watching me. I just wanted the pain to stop, but I was still determined to not look to God for help.

The Reverse Effect

I resigned! I just let go of consciousness in hopes of getting relief from the pain. And that's when the voice popped into my head again.

This time the voice was laughing at me saying, "Oh, what's up to Mr. Tough Guy, Mr. Warrior, Mr. Invincible?" I said to the voice, "What the f*#k! I don't need help." I felt I would rather die than ask for help. However, the voice kept laughing, and then there was an eerie silence.

This is hard for me to put into words because the message didn't come in words, but more like short video scenes. At the edge of my consciousness, I simultaneously heard the man holding my head, counting and trying to bring me back to consciousness... "3, 4, 5..."

The message was that if I wanted my life to change, I had to be willing to make the changes in my life. Scenes of multiple future events flashed in my head. Like I said, these visions are hard to explain in words. "... 8, 9, 10."

I saw years of possibilities flash in front of my eyes. One possible future stood out, and it scared me. The future me was me but was not me. It was like looking at myself but knowing I was different. I was not fueled by anger or rage. Instead, there was peace and purpose. As I watched this alternate version of me, I could also see faith and determination. "... 11, 12, and 13."

I could feel myself being drawn back to consciousness, like in the movies when dead people are being brought back to the light. I then opened my eyes and realized I was still in a f*#ked up situation. I screamed out in pain. Twenty minutes later, the police arrived, and I was given morphine and

*loaded into the ambulance. Now, it was time for the real pain
to kick in. This was the pain of looking at the person I had
become and the people I had hurt along the way.*

*Quickly, the paramedics loaded me into the ambulance and
rushed to the hospital. In the emergency room, I was given
morphine and was prepped for surgery. I remember the
nurses saying I had a 90° rotation break of the tibia and
fibula (shinbone) which means the distance from my knee to
my ankle looked like an L shape. As I lay on the surgery bed,
I had a brief moment to think about what just happened. Then
I heard the doctor say count back 10 to 1. I said, "10, nine..."*

*When I woke from surgery, I felt very little physical pain,
but I knew something was different, physically and mentally.
For the past ten years, I'd lived with a death wish. Now I
was actually happy to be alive. Up until this point, I never
considered living past the age of 30. I was hoping to go
out like a "G," and die in the streets. I made a lot of stupid
decisions based on this perception. Now I was starting to
wonder what would happen if I did get old.*

Nevertheless, I was still an angry and bitter person. The more I
looked at my life, the more bitter I became. Though I knew those
13 seconds had happened, I didn't know how to make any sense of
it. At the time, the whole event was outside of my understanding.
Still, I was not buying into the "God" thing. But, I couldn't deny that
something was changing within me even though I didn't know what
that something was.

PERSPECTIVE:

*The difference between depression and happiness is a purpose.
"Perspective"*[100]

Chapter 9

Healing and Growing

In my experience, unlocking your real potential is unlikely unless we break the binding chains of our past. Healing and growing is an inside job that cannot be accomplished from the outside. True success will not be achieved as long as sadness rents more space in your head than joy. On the journey to becoming the strongest and most creative you, you must detox. I'm talking about detoxing mentally, emotionally, physically and spiritually.

There are many ways of healing, often requiring a combination of processes. One tried-and-true method is **prayer**. Scientists and psychologists have performed multiple studies to test how prayer works. Time and time again, they have witnessed positive results they cannot explain. Though unsure how it works, they cannot deny the positive power of prayer as a tool for internal healing.

Unfortunately, most do not reap the benefits of prayer because they want God to do all the work. Everyone knows the verses, "What does it profit, my brethren, if someone says he has faith but does not have works?" James 2:14 (NKJV) and "Thus also faith by itself, if it does not have works, is dead." James 2:17 (NKJV) However, most do not live by these words. I believe it requires prayer, belief in yourself *and* action to succeed.

Praying for positive results while believing you are not worthy of those results, will get you a bunch of nothing. Prayer and self-doubt do not mix, but unknowingly people do it all the time. Consequently, instead of having a call to action, we self-sabotage and close our minds off to the answer. Believe you are worthy and watch how your prayers manifest into a physical reality.

Another method for healing is **letting go.** Yes, just simply letting go, giving a blanket pardon to everyone who has wronged you. This process usually involves the realization that things in the past are over. A blanket pardon does not mean the negative people in your past are not guilty or do not deserve consequences. I am simply saying you are no longer going to give past people or circumstances power over your current and future life.

The key is remembering there's nothing to gain from holding on to regrets, but there's plenty of reward in moving forward. Moving forward will help you to establish a new self-identity (an identity that you control) and provide you with a straight path to break the chains of your past and unlock the doors to your future. Nothing compares to knowing you have control over your destiny. Master your past, and you become the author of your future.

The next method for proven emotional and physical healing is a technique called **guided imagery**. Guided imagery is based on the concept that your body and mind are connected, and you can use this connection to heal your body and mind. Guided imagery is a gentle, but powerful technique that focuses and directs the imagination. One of the greatest cons in history is the lie that our imagination is not real. The only myth in your subconscious mind is the one that you choose to believe. It is almost impossible for the subconscious mind to tell the difference between vividly imagined reality and the physical reality.

Research demonstrates that guided imagery can help you overcome stress, anger, and pain. Here is an example of how your body responds to what your mind imagines. Think of something with a distinct smell or taste such as fish oil. Now imagine drinking the whole bottle. As soon as you visualize drinking the bottle's contents, your face will cringe. The same way that you can imagine something negative and get a bad physical response, you can believe something positive and get a positive response.

Have you heard of the **Law of Attraction,** or the concept of like attracts like? Well, understanding these two concepts will prove vital to your healing and growing. It is this understanding that will enhance your ability to reprogram your thoughts, perceptions, and belief systems. Once you learn to reprogram your thoughts, you are on your way to becoming the master of your past, present and future. Our past only exists in our thoughts and is only real because we allow it to be. You can retrain your thoughts just as you can reprogram your computer.

Let's say your brain is a computer, and your belief systems are the software. This is an analogy to help in the reprogramming of negative beliefs about ourselves. When you want your computer to perform specific tasks, you add, update, or delete individual programs. The brain operates on the same premise; you must upgrade your systems if you want to change. The input determines the output. If you put garbage in, you will get garbage out.

If you allow negative information to be filtered into your brain, the result will undoubtedly be negative. On the other hand, if you let in only positive input, you are sure to reap positive results. It really comes down to a simple formula: garbage in means garbage out. Therefore, you have to input positive programming (knowledge) into your computer (brain) to ensure you are pursuing the achievement of your goals and filter out things that will hinder your progress.

An essential part of healing and growing is learning how to filter out the information that's toxic to our growth. The best part of this process is that we have all the tools that we need to rebuild our brain. For me, this knowledge is very empowering, and learning how to use my brain's focusing system has made an enormous difference. The knowledge of these combined techniques has proven to be invaluable in making significant changes in my life and my coaching.

I'm going to give a quick explanation of how the brain works. Your brain has a built-in filter called the Reticular Activating System (RAS) which is a small, but essential part of our brains. In fact, the RAS is considered the command and control center of the brain and body. It is the brain's information filtering center, and it allows us to pay attention to the things that are important and filter out the things that are not.

Understanding the Reticular Activating System and how visualization works together for success is very important. Through creative visualization techniques, we can train our brains to only focus on the things that are important to help us achieve our goals. This aligns with the principles of the Law of Attraction, but instead there is no mystical hocus pocus. For me, it is a built-in function of the brain that God has given us.

A critical component of healing and growing is changing your beliefs and how you look at the events of your life. This starts with your self-image. Your self-image is your internal image of who you are—the real you, not the person you portray yourself to be or who you pretend to be. It is a complex picture of who you are, what you are capable of, and what you feel you deserve. It's the inner barometer to which, unfortunately, most of us don't pay attention.

Your self-image is built out of whatever you've been told about yourself, your past experiences, and the beliefs that you have developed. If you have a negative self-image, it will be tough to achieve positive goals. When you have a positive self-image you are more resilient, optimistic and a higher achiever. Knowing whether you have a positive or negative self-image requires honesty and courage. No one likes to admit that they feel bad about who they are.

One way to measure your self-image is to take an honest look at your life. How do you feel about your accomplishments? Are you continually criticizing yourself? What are you attracting into your life? What you attract is a reflection of what you think of yourself. Do you feel as if you attract more negativity than positivity into your life? Is your career going in a positive direction?

Take notice of the people you care about, whether friends or family. Do they seem to take advantage of you? Are the people in your life lifting you up or tearing you down? If you find yourself settling for far less than you know you deserve, then chances are you have a negative self-image. There is a positive side to realizing that you have a negative self-image. Remember the adage, "If you know better, you do better." Now that you know, you can start to make significant changes in the way that you see yourself.

Having a positive self-image is vital to overall success and self-fulfillment. People with positive self-images are confident and have high standards. Letting go of the baggage frees up space to put in positive things and create new beliefs about yourself. This can enable you to turn a negative self-image into a positive one. Working in this area will empower you to create your own standards to live by. No longer will you be a prisoner to someone else's version of success and happiness. This is when you truly start to be original. In order to start cleaning house and building your true self-image, learn self-acceptance.

PERSPECTIVE:

Once you know your worth, everything changes. "Perspective"[100]

Chapter 10

Seizing Opportunity

PRINCIPLE 5

Become an opportunist with principles: An opportunist with principles is a person who exploits circumstances to gain immediate and long-term advantage.

Most of us have been taught that being an opportunist is a bad thing. We have been fooled into thinking that an opportunist is someone who takes advantage of people and disregards principles. You can see the word *opportunity* in *opportune*. Both words come from the Latin word *opportunus*, meaning "favorable," which itself is derived from a phrase that describes wind blowing toward a port. Just as the wind helps speed ships toward shore, something that is opportune offers favorable circumstances for accomplishing something or doing something.

The suffix "***ist***" often corresponds to verbs ending in -ize or nouns ending in -ism, denoting a person who practices or is concerned with something, or holds certain **principles**, doctrines, etc. (for example, *apologist; dramatist; machinist; novelist; realist*). So for me, an opportunist is someone who seizes and/or creates favorable circumstances for accomplishing a goal that aligns with their principles. Most successful people are those who are good at seizing opportunity.

I have learned that opportunities exist all around us. Most of the time, we let those opportune moments sail right past us. This is because we have been falsely conditioned to believe that sticking to a plan that is failing is somehow noble. We have been taught that loyalty is going down with the ship, instead of doing everything you can to get yourself and everyone else off the ship safely. Being an opportunist with principle requires courage and creativity.

Remember, it is your direction that will determine your destination. There is a Chinese proverb that says, "The journey of 1,000 miles begins with one single step." But if that first step is in the wrong direction, you will waste a lot of time going the wrong way. Recognizing when you're going in the wrong direction and having the courage to change course is vital for maximum achievement. Experience has taught me that opportunity can be found in the most unlikely of circumstances, even mistakes and failures.

Unfortunately, many people have been convinced that failure is real, and your mistakes are something that can define you. You will be faced with millions of choices in life, so it is inevitable that mistakes will be made. It is said some of the best learning opportunities will come from our failures because that's when we learn what did not work. I believe the key to success is learning how to grow from failure and finding opportunity in mistakes. Unfortunately, I was a slow learner. So, I made a lot of mistakes, and it took a lot of lessons for me to get the point.

In retrospect, I have learned a lot of lessons over the years. The most valuable is to not allow my past mistakes to determine my future potential. Everyone is going to experience failures, and some of those failures are going to be painful. But the more painful the failure, the greater the opportunity to learn. This next "reflection" is one of the biggest tests I'd encountered up until that point because my life was literally on the line.

REFLECTIONS:

The six months following my accident was an opportunity to look myself and reevaluate the direction of my life. Before my accident, I used my physical abilities to intimidate and cause fear in people. Now, with those abilities gone, I found myself having to face the reality of my situation. I was not liked, loved or respected, only feared. Now that I was no longer able to induce fear, I was nothing. Or, at least, this is the reality that I chose to believe.

This was a moment of truly starting over in my life. It was my opportunity to separate from the persona of who I was and seize the opportunity to become who I was meant to be. But I found it challenging to make that separation. I had worked hard and risked so much to establish my identity. It was hard to leave that part of me behind even though I knew there was very little positive in the person who I was, and that nothing good could come from that lifestyle.

This was a time of reflection. I recalled an incident from when I was 19 years old. My friends and I were outside a nightclub, and we got into an argument with some older guys. I was telling one of the older guys that his time had passed, and it was best for him to step aside or get stepped on. Then he pulled out a gun and pointed it directly at me and said, "Clint, you think you are invincible, but if you do not shut the f*#k up, I'm going to shoot your a** right here."

Instantly, I was confronted with a potentially life-changing choice. I had been face-to-face with death on a few occasions, but this was different. This was up close and personal. That guy was about 15 feet away from me, with his gun pointed at my face. At this distance, the chances of missing were slim to none. So, I weighed a few options before I spoke my next words.

My first thought was, "How fearless am I?" My second thought was of the crowd around me. I would look like a coward if I didn't stand my ground. Yeah, my priorities were messed up back then. I thought, "At this distance, if this guy wants to kill me, I'm going to die anyway. If I'm going to die today, I would rather die proving my point."

Now, all these thoughts happened within a matter of seconds. Then I looked at the guy, eye-to-eye, and spoke, "Old nigga, you don't have the balls to shoot me." As we stood there, gazes locked, he aimed the gun in my direction and fired... BANG! For anyone who has ever been at gunpoint, you understand the feeling of time slowing down to super slow-motion and the eerie silence of imminent death.

For a few moments, there was no crowd; there was no noise, it was just me and the gun. Then the next shot rang off... BANG! Everything was then back to full speed, and I could hear voices in the crowd saying, "He thinks he's Superman," and "He's going to get put in his place."

Hearing these words strengthened my resolve. In my stance of defiance, arms folded, the third shot rang off...BANG! As bullets swished across my face, I started to reconsider my position. I wondered, "Is this worth it?" And I decided, "YES, it was."

Remember, I was still suicidal, just not to the point of killing myself by my own hand. At this point, I could see a shift in the guy's eyes and his body language. I could see that looking at him as if he was a joke was taking its toll. This time he lowered the gun at point blank range, and I knew the end was here. He squeezed the trigger, and "CLICK..." With the adrenaline of a thousand years, I rushed him.

This and many other events in my life had become a part of who I was. It defined me when I had no self-identity. If I let that part of me go, who would I be? It was during those months of being disabled that I realized it was this part of me that was the problem. I took a hard, in-depth look at myself and started asking myself difficult questions such as: "Who am I? What and who am I mad at? What have I accomplished with my life?"

I started to consider how I would be remembered if I died on that day. My thoughts were focused on what type of legacy I'd leave for my children. I had to consider what would happen if I lived to be a senior citizen. At the time, I did not have the answers to these questions. But with every fiber of my being, I knew this was an opportunity that I should not ignore.

Believing myself to be strong and brave, I looked at my life and realized that I was everything except that. I had to admit to myself that I was weak and cowardly, and the real reason I wanted to die before age 30 was that I didn't have the courage to face real life. I had to admit to myself that I didn't have the mental durability to truly handle my responsibilities. All the drinking and drugs were just another way to mask the pain of the trials and tribulations of life.

At the age of 26, I had to admit I was a loser and this revelation, above all, was unacceptable. It was not something that I could live with because I hated losing. I was not ready to die, and I definitely did not want to die a loser! I had to gather my courage and face my fears—the fears of my past and the unknown future. In retrospect, I did not know what to expect, how I was going to move forward and how much work it would take. I just knew if I was alive, I could change.

Life is full of opportunities. If you put yourself in front of opportunity's path, it will smack you right in the face. Whatever happens to you in life, you must use it to your advantage. I repeat: *Use everything that happens to motivate, drive, and empower you to success*. Take nothing for granted; appreciate EVERYTHING! Do not let the fear of past or future failures stop you from the pursuit of your dreams. The only foolish mistakes in life are the mistakes that we do not learn from and those that we continue to repeat. Life is about living, and living is about growth and progress.

Sometimes, we can't remember all of the foolish and reckless things we did as a child because we have grown into wise and successful individuals. There are lessons and blessings hidden within our mistakes. However, it is up to us to dig them out. Sometimes the lesson is not going to be spelled out in black and white. You will have to work for it, meditate on it, and pray about it. Be wise and capitalize on your mistakes versus being hindered by them. Use everything and every experience to your advantage. Turn your weaknesses into strengths. "When life gives you lemons, sell lemonade," says writer and philosopher Elbert Hubbard.

One obstacle that I faced was my lack of a college degree. I could have allowed that to hinder me. Instead, I used it to my advantage. I decided that I would be a beacon of hope to others like myself who cannot afford a college degree but have the mentality and skills set to generate independent income. I coined a phrase called "*Application Independent*," which simply means we position ourselves such that we are no longer required to fill out someone else's application for income or approval.

Knowing that I do not possess degrees and certifications has not deterred me from the pursuit of my dreams. On the contrary, it has caused me to focus on a higher level of excellence in business interactions. The luxury of hiding behind a degree or certification is not my story.

My businesses are results-based and client satisfaction driven. I know that if I do an excellent job, have great customer service, and go that extra mile for all of my *The Reverse Effect* clients, my businesses will do well. I am now turning my shortcomings into my blessings as opposed to using them as a handicap. By using the steps and processes of personal development and goal achievement outlined in this book, I'm defeating the odds. I want you to be able to beat the odds as well. If I can overcome all my failures, you can do it as well.

We must always strive to be the master of our circumstances and not allow our circumstances to become our masters. The saying is true: "Nothing comes to a dreamer but sleep." You cannot sit around and wait for an opportunity to come knocking at your door. You have to go out and get it or create it.

Learning to be proactive is vital in order to change your life. Without action, your thoughts are worthless - kind of like potential and kinetic energy. Potential energy (thought) is stored energy. It can be viewed as motion waiting to happen. Kinetic energy (action) is when an object starts moving. In our case, it's when the thought becomes action, materializing into a physical reality.

When we think of achieving big goals such as weight loss or financial and personal success, we want those thoughts to become a reality. But, we have to be willing to put in the hard work. We cannot rely on hopes, wishes and prayers alone. James 2:14-17 (NKJV) tells us that faith without works is dead:

> *"What does it profit, my brethren, if someone says he has faith but does not have works? Can faith save him? If a brother or sister is naked and destitute of daily food, and one of you says to them, 'Depart in peace, be warmed and filled,' but you do not give them the things which are needed for the body, what does it profit? Thus, also faith by itself, if it does not have works, is dead."*

We have to be willing to go out and seize our dreams from the realm of thought and drag them into a physical reality.

PERSPECTIVE:

While the average person is looking for time to rest and chill, go-getters are looking for opportunities to seize. "Perspective"[100]

Chapter 11

Courage and Facing Fear

PRINCIPLE 6

Courage: Mental or moral strength to venture, persevere and withstand danger, fear or difficulty.

The most formidable adversaries of progress are fear and doubt. Fear is a driving force behind a lot of the life-changing choices we do or do not make. Fear is a portable prison; people will carry it with them everywhere they go. It's a self-created barrier to success and a dream destroyer. People governed by fear and doubt filter major decisions through the lens of fear thinking, "What will people think of me? Will I fail or succeed? If I fail, will they think I'm a loser? If I succeed, will they think I'm full of myself?"

There are about five fears that every human suffers from in some form or another. But I have learned that most fears are created within our own minds or are accepted fears from someone else's mind. Either way, the only realities our fears have are the ones that we give them. Once we realize that we have control over most of our fears, we can start to truly live. A wise teacher once said, "Everything you need is already within you."

Five Common Fears:

1. Losing a Loved One

2. Criticism from Our Peers
3. Being Financially Broke
4. Being Lonely
5. Death

There are a host of fears holding people back from transforming their lives and achieving their dreams. Conquering fear is often easier said than done, but it is a goal that is achievable. There is this misconception that courage means you do not experience fear when, in fact, courage only manifests in the presence of fear. Many courageous people speak of how scared they were while performing courageous acts. I, for one, would not want to associate with someone who was truly fearless because they will get us both killed. Fear is our body's natural early warning system to probable danger, but we do not have to be a slave to it.

John McCain survived five years as a POW (prisoner of war) during the Vietnam War. His fighter plane was shot down by Russian missiles. As a result, he suffered broken arms and legs. He was tortured for more than five years after his capture. When he was offered to be released early, he refused. He focused on something greater than his fear, and that took courage. About courage and fear, he says, "Courage is not the absence of fear, but the capacity to act despite our fears." Surviving his ordeal, he became a United States Senator and ran a close race behind President Barack Obama in his candidacy for President in 2008.

As for myself, my battle with fear was long and tough. However, I endured and learned to master it. Although I am no longer hindered by it, I still experience fear. But I do not let it stop me from progressing and achieving my goals. This is because my purpose or reason for achieving these goals is stronger than the fear. In this chapter, I will continue to give examples of how fear almost killed my spiritual, emotional, and personal growth. I will also give examples and tools that I've used to overcome and master my fears.

(Before I start this next paragraph, I want to put out this disclaimer: my father was not abusive intentionally. Most pre-generation X parents were taught, "Spare the rod and spoil the child." As a result, we got good old-fashioned ass whippings that by today's standards would be considered abuse. Also, neither of my parents knew about the sexual abuse until the publishing of this book).

REFLECTION

Growing up, I was taught to be tough. So, from the outside looking in, people thought I was living a fearless or reckless life. In actuality, I was running from my fears. The physical abuse that I had suffered as a child gave birth to low self-esteem, a negative self-image, and anger. As a victim of sexual abuse, I often wrestled with the questions, "Was it my fault?" and "Did I deserve it?" and "How is it that the people who are supposed to protect me and keep me safe would take advantage of me this way?"

As a child, I knew I had done things that required disciplinary action, but I could not wrap my head around the idea that those actions required water hoses and cable cords as a form of punishment. I began to believe that extreme violence was the best way of getting people to comply to my way of thinking. Then I wondered, "When I grow up, will this be the way that I treat the people I love?" I was confused by these questions, and it made me feel ostracized, weak, and vulnerable. As a teen and young adult, I vowed that no one would make me feel that way again.

For years, I walked around an angry person feeling like I always had something to prove. I felt I had to show everyone, but most importantly, I had to show myself that I was no punk and that I was not weak. The result of this self-destructive mindset was numerous confrontations with my community and ultimately the law. Between the ages of 15 and 16, I was in and out of the juvenile justice system. By the time I turned 17 years old, I was sentenced to Florida State Prison.

As crazy as it may sound, something inside of me was actually happy to be going to prison. To me, this was my opportunity to prove that I was tough enough to make it on the streets and in prison. I wanted to prove to myself and everyone else that I was no victim and that I'd do whatever it took to prove that point! It seemed I was always angry and looking for a fight; I had a huge chip on my shoulders. It would be years before I realized that the real battle was with me and within myself.

Making positive life changes is not something that happens overnight, and I'm definitely no exception to that rule. My recovery time from the accident did provide me with the opportunity that I needed to take a long hard look at myself. What I saw, I did not like. God had provided me with an opportunity to change the course of my life. In recalling those 13 seconds, I believe I was given a glimpse into my future or possible future. I saw a vision of an option if I proceeded down a path of faith.

(Trust me, for years this sounded crazy to me as well).

Also, in those 13 seconds, a list of 13 changes that were going to happen was revealed:

The Reverse Effect

1. I would be a healer.
2. I would be a mentor.
3. I would be a positive role model.
4. I would be a motivational speaker.
5. I would be inspirational.
6. I would live a drug- and alcohol-free life.
7. I would be told that I'm blessed.
8. I would empower and motivate people in places my feet have never been.
9. I would have an empathetic heart.
10. I would help others' light to shine.
11. I would be a leader.
12. I would write books that would help people.
13. I would start a program to help people become their best selves.

I feared to take this path because I feared failure. There was not one thing on that list I even considered to be possible. Actually, I wrote this list down and shared it with a couple of friends. The last time I went to prison, I lost this list. On the original copy, I had written at the bottom, "I do not believe this vision because it is not who I am."

The third step is **transforming the mind**. This is where the meaningful action is taken to not only battle our fears but to vanquish them all together. We have to stop looking for ways to validate why we cannot accomplish a goal. We have to reprogram our perspective on failure and realize that our inability to accomplish a goal doesn't mean that we have failed. It actually means that we understand what will not work. With this information, we can clearly see what steps are necessary to continue progressing toward achieving our goals. In psychology, there is a term called neuroplasticity that applies here.

Neuroplasticity allows the neurons—nerve cells—in the brain to compensate for injury and disease and to adjust their activities in response to new situations or to changes in their environment. This implies that through action, we can change the way we think on a cellular level.

The fourth step is **meditation**, a valuable tool with multiple benefits. For me, meditation is simply the settling down of my thoughts. It is something that I try to do at least twice a day, 10 minutes in the morning when I wake up and 10 to 20 minutes in the evening before I go to sleep. Meditation helps increase self-awareness, reduce stress levels, improve concentration, and clear your mind to increase clarity and focus. Once we have clarity, focus, and purpose in our lives, it becomes more difficult for obstacles to derail us from our journey of becoming the strongest and best versions of ourselves.

Overcoming fears will require courage. I do not believe that we are born courageous, rather that courage is something that is developed over time. As we are unique individuals, so is our uniqueness in the speed at which we can develop courage. One surefire way to develop your courage is through accomplishments. You must do things and complete the tasks that you set for yourself. When we envision our future goals, it is an act of faith and requires courage because it is venturing into the unknown. It is the fear of the unknown that often will be our greatest obstacle.

PERSPECTIVE:

Without fear, courage doesn't exist. "Perspective"[100]

Chapter 12

The Strength of Purpose

PRINCIPLE 7

Understanding your "Why" gives you the ability to move beyond the how what or when.

The strongest weapon we can develop to battle fear and stagnation is our purpose. Most people go their whole lives never realizing their purpose. Seeking and finding your purpose should be a major goal in life. Why? Because when you find it, it will illuminate your path to success and personal fulfillment. Our purpose gives us the strength to complete major goals. The very act of selecting a definite purpose and making a plan for accomplishing it is often more than you need to snap you out of the feeling of negativity and stagnation that you experience in life.

On the journey of personal growth and development, we will often find ourselves walking alone. The sun will not always be around to illuminate our paths. This is because people tend to act as they have been conditioned by parents, society and religious institutions. Sometimes, there's going to be darkness and isolation as a result of walking in your purpose. In those moments, our purpose is the guiding light that will help see us through. If you truly want to achieve big goals, your reason for achieving has to be greater than the goal itself.

In chapter one, I mentioned that having a dream and a purpose are not always the same thing. Occasionally, your dreams and your purpose can even be at odds with each other. I would never discourage someone from following their dreams because when you can make your dreams and purpose align, it is a beautiful thing. But I would caution them to make sure that the dream they are pursuing is, in fact, their own and not someone else's.

It is common for our dreams to originate during childhood or at a state in life when we do not know ourselves. Therefore, we can repeatedly find ourselves pursuing someone else's dream for us such as our parents or society. For example, The American Dream is a reality made up by someone else, a reality that most Americans chase. Dreams are goals that we set for ourselves for personal gratification. Your purpose is a force that helps you overcome any obstacles. The pursuit of a dream can lead to the loss of self, because of the selfish nature of personal dreams.

A dream can be related to purpose, but it is more likely connected to your desire for something you would like to achieve. A purpose is your reason for doing something and even though these two sound similar, they are quite different in nature. Your purpose is your call to serve and in some cases your reason for being. Finding your purpose brings meaning and satisfaction to your life. I have learned that following my purpose has not been easy, but it is well worth following. When we follow our purpose, things just feel right. You know, life has a certain flow to it.

Developing your life's purpose is vital to overall success. So vital that most people live a life of unfulfillment when they do not feel they are pursuing something meaningful, or purposeful. When you are doing something that you feel you are meant to do, the effort that you apply toward success is no longer viewed as work. You can easily find yourself putting in 12 to 15 hours of work a day and still feel as if you have wasted time. This is the power of working within your purpose. The real skill is developing the ability to create purpose in anything you feel that you need to do.

As a matter of fact, when other people think that you're grinding and putting in hard work, you might even have a sense that you are slacking off or that you could have done more. Having a purpose is imperative to overall success. Becoming successful requires effort, tenacity, perseverance, and faith.

When you have a purpose, you realize that there will be failures, and you will sometimes find yourself alone. However, when you are serving a purpose, overcoming these hurdles will strengthen and make the journey well worth the struggle.

You see, having a purpose gives the vision and direction one needs to take meaningful steps in the right direction towards achieving whatever it is you want to achieve. A purpose can also give us the feeling that we are part of something bigger than ourselves. Having direction gives one a sense of contribution. When you feel that you are contributing to something or someone, you ultimately feel better about yourself.

We humans are social creatures, and a lot of the goals that we achieve or do not achieve, is heavily connected to our social circle. We want to belong. We want to be a part of something bigger and better than ourselves. This is why a lot of personal and financial success is dependent upon services that you provide to someone else. No one wants to be alone. It's against our nature to want to be in isolation. Frequently, after we've been in bad relationships and have been hurt and disappointed, we think that we prefer to be by ourselves. However, we still find ourselves giving love another try.

REFLECTIONS:

Six months after my accident, I had a lot of pent-up anger. I was angry because I felt people had taken me for granted, and I had lost their respect. Still, very much at odds with spirituality and my place in the world, I found myself drinking hard alcohol and using cocaine almost every day. For the first time in a long time, my confidence had been shaken. I felt as if I was being deconstructed and slowly losing a sense of who I was. The Clint I had created for the past decade was slowly dissolving.

It seemed no matter how hard I tried, nothing that I was doing was working. I was doing the same things that I had done before, but now nothing seemed to be working. I used the same method of selling drugs that I had always used, but it was like I could not turn a serious profit. I kept searching for the strength to maintain the gangster persona that I had built, but it was no longer there. My heart just could not get into it anymore. It was like I was operating on autopilot. The anger that fueled my past seemed to be drying up.

I continued this way until, when I was 28 years old, I was arrested for felony manufacturing and distribution of illegal narcotics. Though I was able to make bond, I knew that this was potentially my last strike with the justice system. To make things worse, two months later I was involved in a physical altercation that resulted in me being stabbed twice. One of the wounds was about two inches from my heart, and the other one punctured my side. It seemed the more I resisted my calling, the more difficult it became to move in the opposite direction.

The funny part of this situation was right before the stabbing incident, that voice in my head said to me, "I suggest you stay home this afternoon." I laughed and went out anyway. As my friend was racing me to the hospital for the stab wounds, I could feel a presence over me. I heard a voice asking, "Why?"

There were no words to describe it. I remember thinking to myself that I was wasting opportunity after opportunity. My decision at that moment was clear. No matter what, I would be accountable for my own actions. I decided that if I lived through that incident, I would live a more meaningful life. I wanted my life to have a purpose. That decision was the beginning of my journey to a more purposeful life.

It seemed the harder I fought my purpose, the worse things got for me. It was like for every five steps forward, I would lose eight steps. But in retrospect, a lot of that forward-backward movement proved to have a meaning. Making it harder for me to move forward in a negative direction caused me to look inward and ask some hard questions. Even now, I often wonder if I did not go through those events and learn from the mistakes I made, who would I be? Would I have found the courage to pursue my purpose in life? Would I have left the Street Life? Would I have been the author of this book? Would I be the Clinton M. McCoy who I am today?

At the core of my being, I do believe most of these experiences were necessary to forge the drive, determination, and a sense of purpose that I have to succeed. On the other hand, I do question the reasons for so many obstacles because there were too many casualties, too many burnt bridges, and too many relationships lost. Ironically, it is the consequences of my bad choices that propelled me to fulfill my purpose. It's like a roaring furnace burning inside of me, screaming, "I will do better! I will be the best that I can be! I will not be remembered as a failure!"

My purpose has many layers and dynamics, some of which are revealed to me on a need-to-know basis. I describe the journey as a series of lessons and tests. Don't confuse this with trials and tribulations. It's more of a worthiness that's acquired through growth and understanding. I compare it to the Bible verse that says, "Study to show yourself approved." The more I learn about my true self and the value of service to other people, the more doors open for me. I once read that people who study others are wise, but those who study themselves are enlightened. To know yourself is the beginning of finding your purpose.

Pursuing your purpose will elevate your life to limits only you can imagine. This is the way to inner peace, fulfillment and truly reaching life's potential. Dr. Elisabeth Kübler-Ross, psychiatrist and recipient of more than 15 honorary doctorate degrees, said, "The most beautiful people we have known are those who have known defeat, known suffering, known struggle, known loss, and have found their way out of the depths. These persons have an appreciation, a sensitivity, and an understanding of life that fills them with compassion, gentleness, and deep loving concern. Beautiful people do not just happen." So, let's understand ourselves, hear our calling, serve our purpose, and control our destiny!

PERSPECTIVE:

To see a person without a purpose is to see a person sleepwalking. *"Perspective"*[100]

Chapter 13

Intentions, Feelings, and Actions

Most challenges and setbacks come as a result of being unclear about where you are going and what you want to accomplish. Having clear intentions is a significant aspect of transforming your life, goal achievement, and financial success. We tend to think that only our actions matter and do not consider the intentions behind the action. However, our thoughts and feelings also matter. They often are critical to our desired outcome. I am sure you have heard the phrase, "It is the thought that counts." Your thoughts and feelings are energies not governed by three-dimensional space or the fourth dimension of time. It is your thoughts and feelings that are the magnetic component of the law of attraction.

Most people are judged on and driven by their intentions which are fueled by our feelings. They are the driving force behind our actions and often govern the amount of effort we put into achieving our goals. I have learned that negative intentions and positive goals will cancel each other out, leaving you unfulfilled. You will get an identical outcome when you set out to achieve positive goals, fueled by negative emotion. Remember, like attracts like. So, you must be what you choose to accomplish, and this takes a certain level of personal accountability. *Proverbs 4:23 ESV* states, "Keep your heart with all vigilance, for from it flow the springs of life."

When you want to activate the law of attraction, there must be alignment and congruency between what you want, who you are, and what you do. Everyone is equipped with the ability to both succeed and fail. Most people do not succeed because they lack the desire to achieve. Most people fail because they have not been taught the three principles of success. Real success is not rooted in the quality of the plan but in the energy we put behind the plan that increases the chances of success.

People have been taught a lot of different methods and techniques of goal setting. The truth is there's a difference between knowing how to set goals and actually achieving one. In fact, the majority of people do not meet most of the goals they set, no matter what method they use. I believe that there are three factors more critical to goal achievement than the method you use to set your goal. I am going to call these components my X-factors of goal achievement.

X FACTOR 1: **Sincerity**

In most cases, people set their goals halfheartedly. One example of half-hearted goal setting is the New Year's resolution. Unfortunately, most New Year's resolutions do not last past February. According to U.S. News, approximately 80% of resolutions fail by the second week of February, so the odds are against you. We all have experienced this at some point in our goal achievement lives. Most of the time, these goals are more like wishes instead of actual goals.

Those who make New Year's fitness resolutions have a weight loss goal they would like to achieve, but their hearts are not entirely into it. They definitely are not clear on what it will take to accomplish their goals. In psychology, they call this the Planning Fallacy. *First proposed by Daniel Kahneman and Amos Tversky in 1979, this is a phenomenon in which predictions about how much time will be needed to complete a future task display an optimism bias and underestimate the time required.* As a result, they fail to create a clear picture of how they will accomplish their goal. They only envision the end of the journey and fail to take into account the hard work, diet adjustments, and the ups and downs of a fitness journey.

Another example is having goals set for you by someone else, like a deadline at your job. Let's say you have a job in sales and you have to meet a quota by the end of the month. As it turns out, this month, you are selling a product that you don't really endorse. Despite your best efforts, you cannot put your heart into it. You work overtime to push yourself to the limit. You give it your best shot to achieve the target deadline, but you still fall short of your goal. In most circumstances, you meet your goal with far less effort, but because your heart was not into it, you fell short.

A third example is the "you should be doing" or "you should have" goals. These are the goals often set for you by family, friends, and society. Most people fail at achieving these kinds of goals because, again, their hearts are not in them. Often, there is no passion for these types of goals. Even when people succeed at these goals, they do not achieve a sense of satisfaction or fulfillment.

X FACTOR 2: **Being Precise**

Defining your goals with precision and crystal clarity is a vital part of accomplishing them. Being able to visualize exactly what you want and how you're going to achieve it is crucial. It's not enough to imagine a new home; you also have to include the details which most people don't consider such as paying the bills, doing the lawn, and other maintenance costs. Creating a visual image of all aspects of the house puts your brain into goal achievement mode because you have been specific. Our brain is an image-driven machine. The more detailed the picture, the more driven we are to manifest our vision into a physical reality. Scientific studies show that if you really want to remember something, you have to visualize it.

Visualization is key to achieving big goals. One of the first Americans to practice the technique of creative visualization was Wallace Wattles (1860–1911) who wrote *The Science of Getting Rich.* In this book, Wattles advocates creative visualization as the main technique for realizing one's goals. That's why you hear people say, "You have to see it to believe it." You have to be able to visualize your goals down to the smallest detail if you want maximum results. Visualizing with crystal clarity is necessary to achieve success and to see the goals as if they already exist.

Here is a good visualization exercise: see yourself with a $10K bank statement. Now, for the next 30 days, see yourself going to the bank and picking up that check for $10K. Visualize every detail of the transaction. Now, tell yourself, *I'm going to do everything in my power for the next year to pick up my $10K check from the bank.* Reaffirming yourself fuels that drive and builds that commitment. It molds the subconscious mind until it works on autopilot to make all of your actions fit a pattern that will align with you getting that check. This is one of the benefits of creative visualization.

Visualization is an internal representation of what it is that you want to achieve. However, when you really want to achieve your goals, you have to do more than just visualize. You have to hear it, feel it, and smell it. This is called creative visualization. Visualization is so effective because your subconscious mind cannot tell the difference between something that is real or vividly imagined. Therefore, if you can vividly imagine and put all your heart into achieving that specific goal, your subconscious mind will drive you toward that achievement.

Clarity of vision is being able to visualize exactly what you want to achieve and how you're going to achieve it. Numerous psychological studies show that our brain and memory are driven by visual imagery. Tests have shown that you remember things better when you see them in picture form. However, it's not just visualizing that makes the difference when achieving goals; all five senses must be used. Using all five senses is an effective enhancement to visualization when you are reprogramming your subconscious mind to help you achieve goals.

Sports teams have been using visualization as a technique to help their players improve. It is a potent tool, and numerous studies have supported the positive evidence found in these tests. You may have heard of this basketball study or a similar one with like results. Judd Blaslotto, Ph.D., of the University of Chicago, conducted a study where he split basketball players into three groups and tested each group on how many free throws they could make. After this, he had the first group practice free throws every day for an hour.

The second group visualized themselves making free throws, and the third did nothing. After 30 days, they were all retested. The first group improved by 24%. The second improved by 23% without touching a basketball. The third did not improve at all. Therefore, the players who practiced mentally achieved the same goals as those who practiced physically.

Remember, we are trying to convince our subconscious mind that the reality we created within our mind's eye is the same reality that exists on this physical plane. As a result, when you are trying to visualize your dreams with extreme precision, you want to use sight, sound, taste, touch, smell as well as temperature, texture, and scent. Consistently practicing these techniques makes the vision of your goals more believable to your subconscious mind. You have to form strong beliefs in your mind that you can and will achieve your goal.

X FACTOR 3: **Congruence**

Congruence happens when the goals you set align with who you are. So, incongruence occurs when you set goals that do not fit with who you are. A prerequisite to this is understanding who you are. Most life-changing goals meet with failure because they do not match your self-image. Trying to complete a goal that does not fit with your self-image is like mixing oil and water.

For example, let's say you are insecure, weighted down with baggage from your past and always wait for things to be handed to you. Now, you set a goal to meet someone who is confident, forgiving and a go-getter. You will have a lower likelihood of accomplishing your goal because it is not congruent with who you are. Like the universal law of attraction states, "Like attracts like." Therefore, when you want to accomplish a specific goal, you have to align the qualities of who you are with the qualities of the goal.

Remember, you must be you to do!

REFLECTIONS:

While I was in the hospital recovering from my stab wounds, I decided it was time for me to man up and take action. I realized that there was a bigger plan for me, but I also knew that the plan would only unfold if I took action. Not knowing what my first step would be, I took a moment to look at where

The Reverse Effect

I was in my life. I also knew that to accomplish my dreams, I had to be able to see them first.

In order to do that, I had to start removing obstacles that blocked my ability to see my visions clearly. My first order of business was to not end up in prison again. I knew it was time to change my image. I knew that if I could get enough people within the community to say that I was a changed man, there might be a chance for me to stay out of prison and maybe get probation. I knew this would not be an easy task since I was either feared or hated by most of the people within the community.

The second order of business would be getting a job. This would be my first job since I was 15 years old. I also knew that having a job would not be enough, as I had been to trial four times (won three and lost one), and prison four times. Because of my background, the state attorney was offering me no plea bargain, and I was facing the maximum sentence of 21 years. This meant that I would be at the mercy of the courts.

My next step was to use the school to show that I have potential academically. I figured out all the steps that were necessary and enrolled in college and started taking courses. Since I only made it to the ninth grade in high school, I had to take a lot of rudimentary courses.

At this point, I didn't care; I was just trying to keep myself out of jail. I also knew that I couldn't just attend classes; I had to show that I could excel academically. I learned that you do not have to be the best student to get good grades, but you do have to know how to use your resources. That was one thing that I was very good at doing.

For the last component, I figured that I would have to have other prominent people in the community to speak for me because I knew that speaking for myself would probably not amount to much. One surefire way to make this happen was to give of myself through volunteering. I started doing volunteer work for a couple of charities in my area.

When it was time for my sentencing, I had accomplished my set goals. I had completed two semesters at the local community college with a 3.0 GPA. I had been working on my current job for seven months and received a great letter of recommendation from a supervisor. I had gotten several positive character reference letters from well-known people within the community.

Even though the State argued feverishly for me to get 21 years, the judge granted me a downward departure from the sentence I was supposed to receive based on the Florida point system. I was shown leniency and given two years of probation with six months of weekends in the county jail. I could not believe it. I felt like I had a new lease on life.

Two months later, however, I tested positive for cocaine and marijuana. I was now sitting in jail and on my way back to prison for the fourth time with a 20-months sentence because I violated probation. My intentions had been to beat the system when they should have been to change my way of thinking. I found myself back in the system I thought I had beaten and headed to South Florida Reception Center.

Our intentions give our reality foundation, meaning, and validity. My plan for change was to stay out of jail, to become a positive and productive person. My reasons were external and not internal. I lacked sincerity. When you want to become the strongest version of yourself, you must start on the inside. My focus was changing the consequences without working on the problem. I should've been focused on healing from within.

My actions were not congruent with the outcome I sought. I had gotten a job, enrolled in school, and started volunteering, but I was still using drugs and alcohol. I had not made a real life change because I was again breaking the rules since alcohol and drug use violated my probation. The key is aligning your intentions with your actions so that you will get the outcome that you desire. You will find people taking on certain projects or following certain dreams to make money while thinking that money will bring them happiness.

Often, people who get that money do not find happiness. Instead of starting with the intention of finding happiness within, they search for external methods to bring that joy. In my case, I intended to dodge the bullet. I was straddling the fence, and this produced negative results.

PERSPECTIVE:

When you want to change your life and be happy, you must understand the difference between fixing the things around you and healing yourself from within. "Perspective"[100]

Chapter 14

My Eureka Moment

"The Eureka Effect (also known as the Aha! Moment or Eureka Moment) refers to the common human experience of a moment of sudden, triumphant discovery, inspiration, or insight." These moments can manifest in the most unlikely of situations and, as you will see, my Eureka moment was no different.

Reception centers are intake institutions built for assessing inmate risks to meet and balance security requirements with program needs. Newly admitted inmates are transported from county jails to one of the prison receiving centers where the risk assessment process begins. Upon admission, inmates are processed and evaluated for medical and mental health screenings.

Prison classification specialists develop an individual profile of each inmate which includes the offender's crime, social background, education, job skills, work history, and health and criminal record, including prior prison sentences. Based on this information, inmates are assigned to the most appropriate custody classification and prison. From this initial classification, an inmate's behavior and continuing risk assessments by prison staff will determine security progression through the various custody levels from maximum to minimum security and eventual release. The State of Florida has three reception centers: North, Central, and South Florida reception centers.

REFLECTIONS:

My conviction happened in South Florida, so my first stop was the South Florida Reception Center (SFRC). I spent my first weeks in SFRC constantly asking myself, "How am I back in prison for the fourth time?" I kept coming up with one answer: It's my fault. I looked at the things I had accomplished within the past year, and I was very disappointed. For the first time in a very long time, I was feeling bad. Not just for myself, but for the people who supported me.

I knew I had a purpose that I was not carrying out, and I knew I was wasting my potential. This realization made me angry. It was as if I had found a hole inside myself. I knew that I had the tools and the ability to fill that hole, but I was not utilizing them. I remember sitting in my cell one evening and asking for a sign and some guidance. Then with clarity from within me, I heard, "Why are you always asking for signs when the signs are right in front of you?"

The lagoon incident was long forgotten, but now it was brought back to me in vivid detail. I remember hearing the voice inside me saying, "I was the hand that pulled you up. If not for me, you would have drowned that day." I was reminded of the prayer that I said when I was 15 years old asking, "If you are real and if I mean anything to you, then show me proof." I'm pretty sure that prayer was answered many times over, but it was only as I sat in my cell asking for guidance that I noticed it. The answer was a question:

"Clint, based on the choices and decisions that you have made in life, where should you be right now?" It was at this moment that everything became clear to me. I knew that there

was a path for me to follow, but I also knew it would be up to me to follow it. Also, I knew that I was fortunate to receive a 20-months sentence, of which I would only serve 17. I was advised that if I took the 17 months to strengthen my resolve not to drink alcohol, use drugs, or smoke tobacco products I would be well on my way to live the best days of my life.

Over the past 14 years, I had been trying to do everything my way and things were not working out. So, what do I have to lose? EUREKA! At that moment, I felt reborn! I had a mission to diligently work at becoming the strongest and best version of myself, for myself. I would be my own motivation and would draw the strength that I needed from within.

I went to sleep that night with a sense of peace in my heart. Even though I was incarcerated, this was the freest I had been in the past 15 years. The next morning, I woke up with a clear vision and an understanding of my purpose. Becoming the strongest version of myself meant strengthening myself physically, mentally, and spiritually.

When I arrived in prison, I weighed 140 pounds. Drugs and the street life had ravaged my body. I was spiritually empty with the mentality of a 23-year old. I knew that I had plenty of work to do and before I could help anyone else, I first had to help myself. Being in prison gave me the opportunity to attack all three aspects of personal growth simultaneously. My first course of action was to educate myself in three key areas: mentally, physically and spiritually. It was as if I had an insatiable appetite to acquire knowledge.

Attacking the physical aspect of my personal growth would be the easiest. Since I was raised by a military father, physical fitness had always been a part of my life. I had been weight training since I was 12 years old. Like most young people, my view of physical fitness was about aesthetics and competitive performance. At this moment, I knew that this perspective was a small part of what true physical fitness is about. I started studying Asian philosophies on internal fitness that foster life balance and the philosophical concepts and psychological impacts of Chi Gong, Tai Chi, Taoism, and meditation.

From my own Western culture, I studied the nervous and endocrine systems in overall fitness. In order to grow mentally, I had to break loose from the shackles of previous ideologies and patterns of thought. I would not be a prisoner of confirmation bias. Instead, I allowed myself to be open to all types of information and multiple viewpoints. Not only did I want to think outside the box, but I also wanted to throw the box away. I spent hours in the library studying history and historical culture.

It did not matter if it was Caucasian, African, or Asian history, Western or Eastern culture and philosophical viewpoints. I was interested in all of it. These studies gave me perspective on myself and the human condition. They allowed me to see that the world is far more significant than me, but that I can still serve a purpose. This gave my life new meaning and drive.

The spiritual part of my journey would prove to be the most difficult. It was not just my lack of faith in the unseen, but also my lack of faith in myself. For me, faith is built on the same principles as confidence; both require action. At this point in my life, I hadn't made any real action toward accomplishing my life's purpose and building spiritual faith. So, the only thing I could do was search to understand me.

The Reverse Effect

When I searched for GOD, I found myself. When I found myself, GOD was already there.

As I learned, I grew and began to observe more. Looking at the guys I was incarcerated with; I became burdened with sadness by their state of mind. There was a perpetual sense of learned hopelessness and complacency that seemed to be almost everywhere. A lot of the inmates would talk about change and want to do something different with their lives, but they felt like it would be hopeless and a waste of time putting in the effort. They were complacent in thinking that they were caught up in a system designed to keep them down. They felt breaking the chains of poverty was next to impossible.

I remember getting into a heated debate with an inmate over the effectiveness of learning and expanding your mind while incarcerated. This individual actually stated that "it was foolish." He questioned the effectiveness of learning things about the outside when your physical body is still locked up. I was baffled by this, not because of the way this guy was thinking, but because I used to feel the same way.

Aristotle said, "It is during our darkest moments that we must focus to see the light." My darkest moment was sitting in a prison cell at the age of 30, but at that moment I saw the light. The epiphany that I received at that time was that the light was always there, I only needed to summon up the courage to walk in it. The ability to become more than your circumstances is something that we are all born with. Unfortunately, we are not all taught this valuable lesson. We are the only reason that we have to remain a prisoner to our past.

PERSPECTIVE:

Your success should be measured against the fulfillment of your own potential, not against someone else's, their accomplishments, or the lack thereof. "Perspective"[100]

Chapter 15

Mastering Circumstances

"Circumstances? What are circumstances? I make circumstances," Napoleon Bonaparte declared. Most people allow things outside of them to affect their moods and behaviors while doing nothing to change the situation. Being emotionally affected by external conditions such as what people say or do, often brings needless unhappiness. Imagine how productive you would be if you could stay calm and poised in the midst of whatever is happening in your life. Though this is often easier said than done, it is a skill that can be built and strengthened. This ability is emotional detachment.

Emotional detachment is the ability to have compassion and empathy for others without negotiating your own boundaries. It means not taking things personally, which allows you to keep focused on the bigger picture of achieving your goal. Mastering the ability to detach does not mean your life will be problem-free, or that there will not be difficult times. Instead, it will affect your attitude towards life's circumstances and change the way you react.

Mastering detachment aids you in becoming the master of how you react to life's events. Controlling your emotions during stressful situations is often the deciding factor between taking control or becoming a victim of circumstances. This is not a state of indifference, loss of interest or lack of feeling. People who are indifferent do not care about anything and are usually passive. True detachment is something else. It is an attitude of common sense, open-mindedness, and practical behavior.

Managing your emotions is like controlling your diet. It is the most difficult thing for people to do, so it goes without saying this is not an easy task. This is the skill I used to help me through my last time being incarcerated. It is a skill, some 12 years later, that still requires a lot of work for me. But the simple act of paying attention to my feelings and seeing how they affect my actions has made a world of difference.

REFLECTIONS:

I had been to prison on three prior occasions, and I had hoped I would not return or at least not get caught again and find myself in the same predicament. There were no genuine efforts to rehabilitate me. During my previous incarcerations, most of my time was spent gambling and participating in gang activity. This time was different. I knew deep down inside that I was changing, and because of that, I knew that this would be my last time being incarcerated.

I remained in SFRC for about six weeks. One morning, I was being transferred to Fort Myers Work Camp (FMWC). As a minimum security facility, FMWC houses prisoners with low-level risk and rehabilitates them through hard labor. It was here that I would learn what real hard work was. Within my first week, I received my job assignment working for the Department of Transportation (DOT). There are many different jobs a prisoner can take on with the DOT, and I was assigned one of the hardest jobs: ditch duty.

The Reverse Effect

If you have ever driven down the highway and noticed the guys in prison uniforms working on the side of the road, that's what I mean. I was one of those guys, in knee-high mud and waist-high water shoveling muck out of ditches. The only point of this meaningless task was to make sure that we worked hard, and we did. We worked 10-hour days, four days a week, with only two 15-minute breaks and one 45-minute lunch break.

If you've ever worked in the hot Florida sun, you can understand why I didn't like my situation. But, I also knew that I would not let it defeat me. I decided I would take a seemingly bad situation and use it to my advantage, to make me physically and mentally stronger.

I have a fear of reptiles and bugs. Of course, there was an abundance of many things to fear in those ditches of tall grass and water in the heat. I had long since learned to deal with fear, but I had never practiced the art of detachment. The art of detachment is what helped me not just get through my situation, but it taught me to become the master of my circumstances. Detaching myself from the emotions of my situation allowed me to just do the work and get it done.

My goal was to accept the consequences of my actions and to do the work without complaint and emotion. I was no longer a victim of what was going on around me. I had become the master of my circumstances. Working hard under those brutal conditions taught me to appreciate a lot of things like the fact that I could work, think and feel. I understood that I could learn from my past and plan a future.

If I tell you that during these times I was all smiles and that there weren't a lot of tough days, I would be disingenuous. But I learned to work through it because I always had my "Why?" And, my "why" (the reason for doing what I do) is what empowered me. It was my reason for pushing forward. I refused to be in a perpetual state of hopelessness. There would be days that I would be forced to the brink of exhaustion, but I would not let it show. I refused to be broken because I wanted to prove to myself that I had the inner strength to be whole. I did this day in and day out for the next four months until I woke up one morning and was told that I was being transferred.

Transfers are based on the needs (security, health, education) of the inmate and/or the needs of the Florida Department of Corrections (DOC). The DOC has substance abuse programs at designated institutions throughout the state. These programs offer drug offenders with substance abuse problems help to overcome these situations. I was transferred to one of these programs at Gainesville Correctional Institution (GCI). I had been to many drug programs throughout my criminal career and learned that it was common for drug dealers to say that they were users. This was done with hopes of gaining a lenient sentence.

Most juvenile criminal activity has substance abuse at its core. From a very young age, I learned how to manipulate drug programs, but I never had any interest in integrating the information. I was probably not ready. When someone is not prepared, it doesn't matter how well the message is packaged; they will not receive it. I always felt they were all the same 12-step-based programs focusing on God or support groups as the way to maintain sobriety.

Now, don't get me wrong. I'm not saying that these two modalities are not effective in helping people deal with physical, mental, sexual or substance abuse. However, I do not subscribe to those schools of thought exclusively. It was not long after I had arrived at GCI that I learned that this program was different and that I was unique. It was a 13-months nonfaith-based psychological approach to dealing with addiction, and it didn't try to discredit a spiritual or group-based method of dealing with addiction. Instead, it provided options. Just as with my time at the work camp, I decided I was going to get the full benefits from my experience.

The previous six months of my incarceration steered me in the direction of looking internally for the answers to my problems. I realized that the strength I needed to take control of my life, started from within. Being off drugs allowed me to see things more clearly, and it became easier for me to define and accomplish my goals.

PERSPECTIVE:

My future visions are my current reality because I am a product of the future I envisioned in my past. "Perspective"[100]

Chapter 16

Becoming Truly Free

When most people think of addiction, they think of the physical or the stereotypical addict. From my own personal experience, I learned that chemical dependency could lead to physical, emotional, and psychological addiction. Many stereotypes are brought to mind when thinking about drug or alcohol addicts. People who abuse substances are typically viewed as deviants who don't engage in societal norms like the rest of the population.

They are thought to embody different values than those held in the mainstream. All too often, they are imagined to skirt the edges, refuse to work, drop out of school and prostitute themselves. Some of them may be victims of dysfunctional homes. They are thought to take drugs in the dark, dirty alleyways or squats, rob innocent people, go on binges, or engage in high-risk behaviors. The reality of substance abusers is that the majority of them are just like everyone else.

However, the reality of substance abusers is that the majority of them are just like everyone else. Some of them may be victims of dysfunctional homes. They are parents, children, friends, co-workers, sisters, and brothers. They hold down jobs, have friends, attend social functions and enjoy their weekends. Some fail to manage their addiction and become entrenched in a lifestyle that the stereotypes embody, but many do not. Addiction does not discriminate between rich and poor, young or old. Most substance abusers are what we call functional addicts. These are the addicts that are able to function in society while being chemically dependent. Also, there is a difference between substance abusers and addicts.

Though someone can be an addict and a substance abuser, you can also have an addiction that is not chemical in nature. Most people are in denial of their addictions because they compare themselves to the stereotypical drug user or addict. Addiction affects us psychologically, emotionally and physically. The following are some traits associated with alcoholism, addiction to street drugs, prescription drug addiction, sex addiction, codependency, compulsive gambling, work addiction, and food addiction, etc.:

Self-Medication: An individual uses the substance or external vices to fix situations and feel better. Mistakenly, they believe that they are only using it for social reasons or pain management. But, in fact, it is "helping" them cope with life.

Normalizing: This occurs when a person wants to feel normal because of the shame they feel. In response, this person starts looking for a way to fit in with everyone else.

No one starts with the intention of becoming addicted to anything. My drug addiction was no different. I was not raised in an environment where I witnessed crime or drug use in the home. For the most part, I grew up on military bases. And though I did see alcohol use, I did not view it as a crime or see the negative impact that alcohol can have on a person. At 15 years old, I would have never imagined myself smoking a cigarette, drinking, or doing drugs.

As it turns out, I did all of these things before I was 16. It was like a polar shift. In one short year, my life had turned upside down in ways I could never have imagined. Though I had never used drugs or alcohol in previous years, the experiences that I endured made me a great candidate for addiction once I started. Like most kids, I started getting high for fun, trying to fit in with my peers. It soon became a release from how I was really feeling. Because I was raised to be tough, I had mastered hiding the pain.

I was taught through religion and social beliefs that physical discipline was something that I endured because I was loved. Nevertheless, being physically disciplined with water hoses, extension cords, TV cable cords, and two-by-four boards never seemed like love to me. The sexual abuse by my babysitter when I was 5-years old and a family member when I was 11-years old alienated me. This caused me to feel like an outcast. In those days, there was no one to talk to about these matters because such matters were not talked about. It was difficult as a young teen to make sense of it all.

I felt different from everyone else, and I wanted to feel as if I belonged. I just wanted to be normal. It's funny when I talk to people who knew me back then they tell me how popular, outgoing, and confident I was and how other people wanted to be like me.

Low Self Esteem: Low self-esteem is having a generally negative overall opinion of oneself, judging or evaluating oneself negatively, and placing a general negative value on oneself. This usually can lead to depression, a victim mentality, and lack of change in behavior.

Our self-image is often the determining factor in the decisions we make. Low self-esteem often leads to an unnecessary overreaction, which ultimately leads to lowering personal standards. This leads to accepting circumstances that we usually would not allow. A lack of self-esteem, altogether, raises the likelihood of self-defeating behaviors and the unwillingness to look inward for the answers to our problems.

Grandiosity: Due to lack of self-esteem, people may inflate their sense of importance. This will usually push people away to escape their vulnerability. Sometimes, addicts have the uncanny ability to have low self-esteem while simultaneously believing themselves to be the best at everything.

Anger: If there is a feeling that is expressed, it is usually anger. Most people dealing with substance abuse, or addiction to external vices, tend to have anger and resentment issues. What I've come to appreciate is that it's okay to be angry, but we must learn how to channel that anger for our own good.

As with most external remedies to internal conflicts, drugs offer only temporary relief. The "help" that is initially provided usually turns into another problem that amplifies the harmful effects of the original issues. Instead of providing comfort, external remedies are like a dam—a blockage of the natural flow of positive growth and healing. An interesting paradox is it does nothing to slow the negative impact of internal conflicts within your life. As conflict sits behind the same dam, these negative aspects grow, bursting through and flooding anything good and positive in their path.

Quick-Fix Mentality: Addicts are used to "fixing" their uncomfortable feelings with their addiction. As a result, they expect change to happen fast and have difficulty waiting for progress over time. One of the reasons relapse is so common is that they are unable to withstand the painful and uncomfortable feelings that occur with withdrawal.

Denial: Pretending a situation is not real is a coping mechanism. It is really not about lying, but about a total unawareness that there is a problem. The more severe the problem, the more it is denied.

Controlling: We try to control what people think of us, our environments, our spouse, and our children. However, we rarely want to put any effort to self-control as we are habitually in denial of the reality of our situation.

These traits alone don't necessarily guarantee that one has a problem, but they help us to begin looking at the possibility of a problem. These traits usually develop well before the person starts using drugs and persist long after the person has stopped using the substance because the underlying issues have not been dealt with.

While I was at GCI learning to build and strengthen my problem-solving skills, the program emphasized self-accountability along with accountability to the local community. This community reinforcement approach addresses the person's capacity to deal with life, interpersonal relationships, employment concerns, leisure planning, and social-group formation.

The focus was on developing life skills, coping with internal and external stress, and building skills that allow constructive and productive expression. This self-accountability and non-confrontational approach allowed for self-propelled change. When it comes to addiction, whether it be a chemical dependency or addiction of other natures, people change when they want it badly enough.

Many times, they have to know that they are, and feel, strong enough to face the challenges of change. I prefer an approach that empowers and offers positive reinforcements to one that strips the individual agency (such as admitting powerlessness). These techniques helped to elicit real changes in me. I completed the program and as of May 31, 2002, I celebrated 14 years of sobriety. I was released from prison in October 2003. Not a drink or use of any narcotics. Now, if I say that I've never had the desire to drink or get high since then, I would be being lying. However, what I can say, without a doubt, is that right now I am living the happiest years of my life and have a true sense of control and freedom.

PERSPECTIVE:

The only real failure in life is not trying because of the fear of failure. "Perspective"[100]

Chapter 17

Why Some People Never Achieve Big Goals

There are many reasons why people do not achieve big goals, but the main culprits are misinformation, antiquated processes, and the wrong attitude. We have been taught big success is achieved through single-minded focus, willpower and having a good plan. I have learned that, most of the time, this is not the case. Sure having a great plan, being focused and exercising willpower can make a difference and result in a few success stories. But most successful people have become successful through routine, attitude and association with like-minded people.

You see, it is your routine that creates your habits, and your habits give birth to success or the opposite of success. Building a routine that aligns with your goals will create habits that will make them achievable. Habits are important because they do not require much willpower to be maintained, but habits require a routine for them to be created. Unfortunately, we have been misled on the creation, nurturing and importance of positive habits. Sure you can create a habit in about a month, but without support, that habit will die.

Your attitude determines how high and how far you go, or your altitude. It's our attitude that attracts situations and circumstances that are congruent with the completion of our goals. Maintaining a positive attitude even when circumstances are not going your way increases the likelihood of success. Success and failure go hand-in-hand, and on your road to achieving big goals, there are going to be setbacks. One of the reasons some people never achieve big goals is they never get back up after being knocked down. Life is 10% of what happens, 90% of how you respond, and your attitude is the determining factor.

Our attitude is expressed through personality, and personality determines our conditions. Therefore, if you want to change your condition, it's as simple as changing your attitude. You have to change your personality to attract people who align with your goals. Remember, relationships are one of the most important factors on your road to success. It's this easy: positive relationships = positive success; toxic relationships = toxic results. You cannot attract positive people with a negative attitude.

By using a simple formula, you can make positive changes that are lasting. Anyone can do it; there is no secret to becoming successful and living your dreams. However, there are invaluable principles that are key to goal achievement. It's the changing of conditions around us that facilitates the changes in our lives. And it's the innate ability to create these changes that gives us mastery over our circumstances.

So, before you can start thinking about achieving meaningful goals, you should be aware of some factors that stop most people from achieving success and what you can do about them. There are a lot of books teaching different steps on how to set goals and make life changes. But, the truth is, there's a difference between goal setting and big goal achievement. A great majority of people do not achieve their goals because of antiquated methodologies of achieving success.

As we learned in earlier chapters, our perspectives interpret our reality. We can change that reality starting with our creative mental ability. There is a technique called visualization that can supercharge the goal achievement process. Creative visualization activates the power of your thoughts and subconscious mind. By taking charge of our thoughts, we choose the nature of our perceptions. We decide whether they will be aligned with the completion of our goals or have a negative impact.

Although implementing these techniques will help you accomplish everyday goals such as saving money, meeting someone, or getting a raise on the job, visualization can be used even more effectively when working on meaningful life-changing goals. Visualization will help make your dreams a reality. It puts your mind on autopilot and guides you to goal completion. The more you practice this technique, the better you will become at it and the bigger goals you will achieve.

Mental and emotional congruency makes becoming your strongest and best self easier to achieve. Aligning your goals with who you are is an important factor in achievement. A prerequisite to aligning your goals with who you are is first understanding who you are. Most of our life-changing goals are often met with failure when they do not match our self-image. Don't let this lack of alignment keep you from achieving your big goals. Completing a goal that does not fit who you are as is like mixing oil and water.

Before my last incarceration, I took many steps toward staying out of jail, but I didn't embody the change. I approached it halfheartedly. With an insincere attitude, I didn't align myself with the qualities that it would take for me to stay out of the criminal justice system. My intentions were not aligned with becoming the best version of myself. Sum totally, I lacked congruence, and because of that I ultimately failed in taking control of the direction I wanted my life to go.

Once I truly embraced the change I wanted, I visualized the exact future I wanted to have for myself. I aligned myself with certain character virtues such as courage, empathy, and appreciation. I knew that fortitude would be necessary for me to make my mental reality manifest. I visualized the obstacles and imagined a solution to overcome them.

You now know several factors that stand in the way of achieving big goals. I have shared these so you won't be blindsided by these obstacles. You now have been equipped with the knowledge to make sure those factors will not hinder your goal achievement. Now that you know what can stand in the way of your success, you're ready for the keys to success.

PERSPECTIVE:
There will always be people who do not want us to feel amazing about ourselves. This is, mostly, a reflection of how they see themselves. "Perspective"[100]

Chapter 18

Keys to Success

Some of the keys needed for your key ring of success are:

1. Clarity

2. Knowledge

3. Commitment

4. Courage

Of course, possessing these keys mean nothing if you don't use them. People often fall short of achieving their goals because they do not understand the difference between a desire to achieve and putting in the work. So, before I talk about these keys to success, I want to emphasize the importance of implementation. I'm going to summarize it in three words, "Do the Work."

The First Key that you will need on your key ring of success is **clarity**. Clarity concerning exactly what you want to achieve is very important. You have to clear the clutter to be able to see it, smell it, taste it, breathe it and achieve it. Becoming clear means you are wholeheartedly in the process. When it comes to setting goals, halfheartedness has to become wholeheartedness. It is important to find something that you really care about.

The Second Key that is a must-have on your key ring is **knowledge.** If you want to become a goal achieving machine, you must also become a learning machine. This does not mean that you must go out and seek college degrees. In fact, most successful people have an average level of schoolbook intelligence. You have to acquire the knowledge of the subject or goal that you want to achieve. You must be willing to read, listen to audiobooks, or go to seminars, get a coach or mentor. One hour per day of study in any subject can make you an authority within three years.

Remaining open to multiple perspectives and viewpoints is vital to becoming successful. This mental flexibility will allow you to adapt to changing circumstances and open your mind to new opportunities. I am sure you have heard the phrase *"knowledge is power."* Interestingly, knowledge is not just power; it is also freedom. With knowledge, you can break free of the chains of mediocrity. With knowledge, you can implement strategies, tactics, and processes that will allow you to plot a course and take your life in the direction of your choosing.

You see, knowledge breeds competence, and competence breeds confidence. When you combine competence and confidence, you develop awareness. The higher your awareness, the lower the likelihood that fear will be a limiting factor in your progression toward accomplishing your goals. It's very difficult for true confidence and competence to coexist with fear.

In today's Information Age, acquiring an immense amount of knowledge on almost any subject is quick and easy. We have so many resources to acquire information and devices to put that information at our fingertips. The World Wide Web is like the Alexandrian Library to the hundredth power. We no longer have to seek out some wise guru or give seven years of apprenticeship to some master to learn what the masters know. We can read or listen to audiobooks and take inexpensive online courses that will allow us to learn almost anything we want. Remember, there is no secret to success; anything we want to achieve has already been achieved at one point in history. We can learn success and failure from the best that has ever done it.

The only real obstacles are knowing what questions to ask, learning how to implement the answers and, of course, knowing ourselves. You do not have to be original to be successful. I believe people commonly make the mistake of striving for originality, instead of finding what works and incorporating that knowledge into their plan. When you want to be successful at something, gather the knowledge of the people who were successful in that something before you. Study what successful people think and become committed to the process of becoming successful.

The Third Key that should be on your key ring is **commitment**. There's a difference between being interested in something and being committed to it. When you possess only an interest in something, you tend to do only what's convenient or easy. However, when you are committed to something, you are willing to do whatever it takes to achieve and willing to learn whatever you need to learn.

To not become a victim of excuses or circumstances, you have to decide what it is that you are willing to cut out of your life. You can't expect to achieve goals if you hold on to the strategies, tactics, and processes that prevent you from achieving success. For instance, if you have the goal of making six figures in the next year, you can't hold onto the habit of being lazy. Likewise, if you have fitness goals of losing weight, you can't hold onto bad eating habits. Committing to something new is one of the hardest tactics of change because it usually means giving up something that we have become accustomed to. Letting go of the things that we are used to takes a lot of courage.

Courage is the final and the hardest of the keys to success to obtain because this is not something that you can study. You can't go down to the corner store and pick up a bag full of courage. Courage is something that is built on achieving and is mustered from within. You may have heard the road to success is riddled with failure. I will tell you that failures will definitely happen along the way. When I woke up to the fact that all of my lawn service equipment had been stolen, I knew that the road forward was going to be tough. However, I did not envision it was going to be as tough as it actually was.

REFLECTIONS:

Originally, I did not build my lawn service from the ground up. Even though I had a serious substance abuse problem before I went to prison my last time, I was no novice in the drug trade. Being arrested for violation of my probation, I had the chance to save and bury a nice stash of money. When I was released, I stayed in South Florida for two years. I used the money for education and the opportunity to mend bonds with my four children. Because of my past, it was very difficult, if not impossible, for me to get meaningful employment.

Due to my entrepreneurial spirit, I did not have any intentions of climbing someone else's ladder. I knew that I wanted to be "application independent." I wanted to put myself in a position to be independent of relying on an external source as a means of generating income. After two years, I could see that I had reached the ceiling in South

The Reverse Effect

Florida, and that's when I moved to Jacksonville, Florida to start the next chapters of my life.

When I moved to Jacksonville, I invested $15,000 in building a lawn service. At this point, I had no landscaping knowledge or expertise. I just knew that I wanted to be my own boss. I also knew that this was a business based on establishing a clientele, and I would use the business concepts that I learned towards the end of my career on the street: fairness, quality, consistency, and value.

I fully expected that because I had all this shiny new equipment and salesmen skills that it would not be long before my business took off. I was told that it could take between three and five years to get a business off the ground. I felt I would be the exception to that rule. I was wrong.

Though I was a novice at landscaping, I was fluent in my understanding concepts and principles of success. I knew that knowledge would separate me from the person just cutting grass and the person running a company. In my first year of business, I focused on trying to learn everything I could about landscaping from different types of grass to lawn treatment, to how to do competitive bidding.

The only problem with my plan was that landscaping was just something I was doing to generate income. It was not a passion. Therefore, I did not appreciate my business. In the beginning, I had a pretty poor work ethic, mainly because I already had money set aside. However, after three years of reckless spending, I was almost broke.

That's when I woke up one morning to find all of my equipment had been stolen. This was right at the height of the

2008 recession. With my remaining $1,500, I bought a small self-propelled push mower, a weed-whacker, an edger, a leaf blower, and a couple of yard rakes. As a result of no longer having the equipment to run my business effectively, I lost 90% of my contracts within two months. I was also evicted from a luxurious 3 bedroom apartment and had to rent a room to prevent being homeless.

Within two months, I could no longer afford to pay my car insurance, so my license was suspended. Every time I drove my truck for work, I was taking a chance of getting arrested. I also defaulted on my student loans. Almost simultaneously, my first winter hit and income from a lawn service was next to nothing. I was forced to go out and get a fast food job at Kentucky Fried Chicken (KFC).

Typically, I could only get a maximum of roughly 30 work hours per week, and I had three child support payments to come out of that check. This would leave me with hardly any earnings remaining. I remember that there were times when I had to make a decision between putting gas in my truck and getting something to eat. That KFC job was both a blessing and a lesson for me. Making money had always been easy for me. So, up until this point, I had never really appreciated the struggle. With the economy being the way that it was, no one had to give an ex-convict an opportunity, and many didn't.

I remember applying for a landscaping company that would not hire me because I had a mouth full of gold teeth and a background. This battle for survival went on for about another year. I went from spending $2,000, as an afterthought, to appreciating the value of an extra $50.

The Reverse Effect

However, this part of the story is not about appreciation; it's about courage.

The average person might think these are everyday struggles in life, but remember that three years before this setback I had saved over $100,000. The only reason I left the drug game is that I wanted something different for my children, myself, and my future. I felt that I had a purpose to serve. I could've easily gone home, saved $30,000 in six months and come back to Jacksonville with a fresh start, but I did not. I kept pushing toward the fulfillment of my purpose in life. I will admit it was difficult knowing that I could easily make fast money being that I was always solicited by people from my old lifestyle. The temptation was inviting.

I remember one time at the beginning of the winter, I simply prayed, *"God I don't know if I can go through another winter like this."* I was sitting in my truck, one evening, with tears on my face, thinking negative thoughts. I did not like my job, my lawn service was slow, and I was tired of struggling. I was seriously considering getting back into the drug game. I figured it would be easy to grab a package from Miami and take it down to Key West for some fast money. I calculated it would take me 60 days to make $15,000. With that money, I could go back to Jacksonville, quit my minimum- wage job and rebuild my lawn service.

While in my feelings, I decided to say a prayer. That prayer was immediately answered. God said to me, *"Where is your faith? Where's your courage? You have come too far to turn back now."* Two things I knew I had at that moment: my faith and courage, and knowing this gave me direction again. I decided I was going to move forward and not backward. Less than two days later, I woke up to a phone call from the same landscaping company that would not hire me a year ago. They were offering me a supervisor's position giving me a $5 increase in hourly pay, plus overtime options.

It is a common occurrence that people give up on the journey right before the sun comes up. It takes courage, commitment and clarity of vision to keep pushing forward when it's easier to give up. The road to success is going to be full of ups and downs, but you must keep pushing forward. Applying these keys to success will unlock your potential and open the doors to the future you desire.

PERSPECTIVE:

Sometimes after the storms of life have passed, and the sun starts to rise, you will notice that rain washed away a lot of dirt (negative people). The wind blew away a lot of the trash (negative thoughts), and the lightning provided just enough light (hope) to help you see.

Making it through life's storms builds your faith, strength, character, and self-confidence. After a while, you learn to smile in the face of dark clouds because you know that with the coming sun, there will be a stronger and better you. ***"SMILE"*** *"Perspective"*[100]

Chapter 19

Strategies, Practices, and Processes

In the previous chapters, we talked about how principles are fundamental to achieving big goals and successfully transforming your life in a radical way. I highlighted seven fundamental principles:

1. Broaden Your Perspective

2. Develop Effective Mindsets

3. Self-Acceptance

4. Self Forgiveness

5. Courage

6. Become an Opportunist

7. The Power of Purpose

I also stated that courage, clarity of vision, perseverance, commitment, and knowledge are necessary keys to achieve big goals. Now, I want to talk about the active components of becoming successful. Without action, nothing happens! You must have an effective plan of action if you want to be successful at consistently achieving goals.

Now, I want to focus on the three active components of success: The overall Strategies, Tactics and Processes (or routines) that you're going to implement. The word "strategy" comes from the Greek word "ΟΡQARYMÍA strategia" or commander. Like a great commander, a strategy gives overall direction for an initiative. A strategy is a planned course of action designed to move you from point A to point B efficiently and effectively. The strategy is the "what" part of the equation that will help you answer the question, "What are we trying to accomplish and what resources will be needed?" Strategy generally involves setting goals, determining actions to achieve the goals, and putting things in place that will get the job done. An effective strategy takes advantage of resources and implements plans to deal with potential obstacles. Strategies should be designed to increase the overall likelihood of success. Your strategy does not specifically say how you will arrive at this end, but it gives you the overall vision you need to succeed. To effectively increase the likelihood that your strategy succeeds, you have to implement good tactics.

The word tactic comes from the Ancient Greek "ranrɔný taktike," meaning "art of arrangement." According to Sun Tzu, "*Strategy without tactics is the slowest route to victory.*" Tactics are the actions behind the strategy or how you are going to complete whatever it is that you need to do. Your strategy is the large-scale plan you will follow to make the dream happen. If you have strategy without tactics, you have a thought without action. Your tactics are the specific actions and sequences of actions you will use to fulfill your strategy. Thought without action equals nothing.

If you have more than one strategy, you will need different tactics for each. This is why focusing on one thing at a time is the most effective way to achieve big goals, though this is not the only path to success. Naturally, the more components you have to any mechanism, the more difficult that mechanism becomes to operate. The same mechanics apply to goal achievement.

Let's say you have multiple goals you want to achieve, the first being to put yourself in a position to ask for a raise. Your second goal is becoming physically and mentally fit, thereby increasing your personal value. Overall, these goals align with personal investment and increase your overall value, both in the workplace and in your personal life. You can have a strategy that's congruent to the completion of both of these goals, but they require different tactics.

For the first goal, some of the tactics you might use are the assessment of your worth, practicing salary negotiations, and asking for an endorsement. In the workplace, performance might get you to the door, but relationships get you through the door and climbing up the stairs. So your tactics are going to involve finding the people who align with achieving your goals and identifying those who are toxic. By "toxic" I mean people who cannot help you advance, whether they are good people or not.

You attack the next goal of becoming physically fit by becoming knowledgeable of what it takes to meet your fitness goal—signing up with a personal trainer and setting aside time for your workout sessions. This part (tactic) of the process involves getting the necessary equipment (i.e., the tools, people, and information needed to achieve the goal). This is vital. Often, we set off to achieve success without the proper equipment which is kind of like going fishing without a rod, hook or bait.

Next, you will look into ways to improve your self-image via Facebook, YouTube, or the Internet. While having a good strategy and developing effective tactics are essential to achieve your big goals successfully, you will often fall short if you do not commit to an effective process. A lot of people do not achieve their goals because they fail to execute their strategies and tactics properly. This often happens when the process part of goal achievement is not aligned with your strategy and tactics.

The process part of achieving a goal is like the glue that holds everything together. You can have great strategies and tactics, but if you don't implement them effectively, everything will fall apart. You see, the process is the habits, rituals, and implementation of tactics that will enable you to execute your strategy successfully. Another key factor often overlooked, but important to the process, is the ability to remain focused. Remaining focused is often under-valued, but it is an essential component of successfully implementing your tactics.

Focus is the ability to center your attention and energy on a specific task, object, or activity for a sustained length of time. The biggest reason people fail at achieving their overall goals is that they take on too much too soon. When you start setting goals, you may see many things that you want to accomplish, so you start setting goals in all areas.

The problem with this is that you have a fixed amount of time and energy. If you try to focus on many different goals at once, you can't give individual goals the attention they deserve. Instead, use the "quality, not quantity" rule when setting goals. Work out the relative importance of everything that you want to accomplish over the next six to twelve months, then pick no more than three goals to focus on. Remember, success rests on focusing on just a few things at a time. If you limit the number of goals you're working on, you'll have the time and energy you need to do things really well!

PERSPECTIVE:

Real confidence built from experience is not broken by doubters or shaken by disapproval. When you know who you are, what others think really doesn't matter. "Perspective"[100]

Chapter 20

Tips for Success

For most of us, becoming successful is a very important part of our life goals. Therefore, I'm going to point out some steps that will drastically increase your successful outcome in any endeavor you choose to undertake. To take full advantage of these steps, you must first define what success means to you. For me, success has more than one component. I believe that success is not just based on materialistic gain, but more importantly, it's about self-fulfillment. Decide what success means to you, and get started!

A key variable that is required in accomplishing anything is finding goals that you can be passionate about. The first step to understanding your passion is self-discovery. You have to have a deep understanding of your self-image, limitations, strengths, and weaknesses. Knowing yourself is important because there will be times on your journey of success when the only thing that will be clear to you is who you are and what you want to accomplish.

The clarity of your vision may be your only guiding light when the darkness of doubt is upon you. I would recommend this exercise: don't just ponder about who you are, what you want, and how you are going to accomplish your goal, write it down. Writing exercises will help you see the vision of your success clearer. One of the biggest obstacles standing in the way of some of my success clients was the failure to set clear goals, and understanding the what's, why's, and how's of goal achievement.

SEVEN STEPS TO SUCCESS

Step 1: Answer these questions

1. What do you want to accomplish?

2. Why is accomplishing this important you?

3. How will this achievement help you?

4. Do you have a specific time frame to accomplish this goal?

5. How will you hold yourself accountable for your timeline?

6. What are the consequences if you do not achieve this goal?

7. How do you plan on accomplishing this goal?

The first step of creating a clarifying goal is to figure out what you want to accomplish and how you plan on accomplishing your objective. If you don't know what you want, you can't know what you need to achieve to get there. Knowing the reality of where you currently stand will help you to figure out the best options to take in achieving your goals. It is important that you can clearly visualize and articulate your goals.

Once you have done the first step, it is important to write your goals down. However, this is only the beginning. Articulating your intention is important, but it is not enough. You must execute your goals; take action. I've found that writing down my goals and reviewing them regularly keeps me on track to complete them.

Step 2: Find and define your purpose.

If you carefully completed step one, you should have enough information to start developing an understanding of what your purpose in life is. As shared earlier, developing your life's purpose is vital to overall success. When you are doing something that you believe you are meant to do, your efforts will no longer be viewed as work.

Step 3: Think BIG.

When I say, "Think big," I mean set ambitious goals for yourself. Do not limit yourself to small goals; set unrealistic and seemingly unachievable goals. I compare this to the saying, "Shoot for the stars so that you can land on the moon." The reason that I do not tell people to set realistic goals is that often when we set goals for ourselves, the word realistic is comparable to limitations. I recommend that no one impose limits on themselves based on someone else's reality.

If someone asked me where I see myself within the next five years, my answer is "I only know the direction that I am going, because I feel my potential is limitless, and I will not limit myself by limiting the reality I create within my own mind." Never sell yourself short, and do not set mental limits for yourself. Set ambitious goals. This will help you be supercharged and give you the momentum that you need to propel you over life's small obstacles.

Step 4: Become educated.

Identify your strengths and weaknesses so that you will know what to enhance. Working toward specific degrees is not mandatory, but not excluded. Learn whatever you need to know about what you want to accomplish and anything connected to achieving that goal.

Learn how to use your resources and build assets and personal relationships with others who might be on the same path as you.

Learn how to communicate and sell your vision effectively. There will be times when we may seem alone in our vision, but this is often because we do not place ourselves in the presence of like-minded people. Educate yourself on things like manners, being tactful, and empathetic. Learn how to communicate your feelings and your thoughts to other people effectively. Stay focused on your learning. Do not waste time on unrelated material. If you want to be successful, study successful people. Focus on the psychology of those successful people; learn their mindsets.

Step 5: Prepare to work hard.

This is the part of success that most people shy away from. Today, many people want that quick fix; they want instant success. Many people search online for a secret to success, but there are no get rich quick schemes or overnight successes. Determining the resources you will need to pursue your success helps get you in the frame of mind to work hard.

Although I have obtained personal success and self-fulfillment, I did not acquire it overnight. It often makes me laugh when people judge me as overconfident or arrogant. What they do not know is that I have put in more than 14 years of work, just to get my life going in a positive direction.

I have put myself in a position that, barring death, I am in control of my own destiny. I cannot conceive of any goals that I will not be able to accomplish. Believe that you are on a mission. If you're hoping, wishing, praying, or even expecting success because you think it is your due, you will find yourself repeatedly failing to achieve your dreams. Be ready to work.

Step 6: Never give up.

You must have the courage to keep pushing forward. You have to remember that things are not going to be easy. That is why I like to choose empowerment over just being motivated. Motivation and willpower alone are not enough to keep you pushing forward. Motivation will get you going, but it is that intestinal fortitude that will keep you moving after the initial surge of excitement fades away.

When you read biographies of successful people, you will find an underlying theme in all of them. That theme is persistence and perseverance. In his biography, Tyler Perry explains that his plays were rejected by everyone for the first six years. But he kept pushing forward, and look where he is now! Believe it or not, the human brain processes more information from our failures than from our successes. That's why people often say that you learn more from your losses than you do from winning. So, be prepared to have some losses and make some sacrifices. Step six prepares you for the rough times.

Step 7: Master your emotions.

You have to learn to master your emotions. You have to be willing to think before you act or speak. Practice detachment. Even though we are guaranteed freedom of speech and the right to self-expression, it is naive to think that we should exercise those rights whenever we choose. Think through your expressions and the possible impact they can have before giving in to an emotional response.

A lot of people in today's society have failed because of this false sense that they can express themselves whenever and however they want. Learn to be tactful and master self-control, and you will find that team-building will become easier. Again, there is no secret to success. But if you apply these strategies and tactics, you will find that accomplishing any set goal will become easier.

PERSPECTIVE:

Woke up one morning thinking of all my past failed relationships and the opportunities that I thought I had missed. Then it hit me... if any of those things had worked out, I probably would not have what I have today. Always trust God's guiding light. "Perspective"[100]

Chapter 21

Going Forward

There you have it, my keys to success, perspectives on goal achievement, and advice for overcoming life's toughest obstacles. I started this book expressing why I wrote it: I've traveled an often destructive road. I want you to learn from my experiences so you can benefit from what I had to learn the hard way. I've been incarcerated, in rehab for alcohol and drug abuse, down and out as some would say. Nonetheless, that was not the end of my story.

In fact, those experiences, as painful as they were, helped to shape me into the person I am today. The good news is that on this journey we call life, your story doesn't have to end where you currently are... It's time to make a fresh start. If you are in a dead-end job, a relationship that's seen better days, or even behind prison walls, you can start over. I know because I did. I made a fresh start in a jail cell. It wasn't easy, but I was able to make something of my life. I was able to continue my education and have a good grade point average. I own businesses that allow me to be application independent. And, I have restored some of the relationships I thought were beyond repair at one time. These are my best days. I work daily to live out what I've shared with you. It's not always easy, but it is possible.

So, what will you do with what you've just learned? Remember, knowledge without action doesn't serve you much. It's now time to act on what you've learned. What change will you make, today? What actions will you discontinue? What new habits will you develop? What goal do you need to set for your future? What purpose do you need to pursue? You can change your mindset to change your life. I've shown you how I transformed my own life. Now it's up to you to do the same for yourself.

"After all, if I can do it, so can you. I'm rooting for you!"

PART II

GOAL ACHIEVEMENT

Goal Achievement: Overview

10 key questions for goal achievement

1. What do you want to accomplish?
2. Why is accomplishing this goal important you?
3. How will the achievement of this goal help you?
4. Do you have a specific time frame in which you want to accomplish this goal?
5. How will you hold yourself accountable for sticking with your timeline?
6. What are the consequences if you do not achieve this goal?
7. How do you plan on accomplishing this goal?
8. On a scale of 1 to 10, how close are you to accomplishing this goal?
9. What obstacles do you see in your way and what can you do about them?
10. In what ways can you use your strengths and talents to help you accomplish this goal?

The first step to creating a goal is to figure out what you want. If you don't know what you want, you can't know what you will need to achieve in order to get there. Knowing the reality of where you currently stand will help you to figure out the best options and steps to take towards achieving your goals. It is imperative that you can clearly visualize and articulate your goals

Once you have done the first step, it is important to write down your goals. The daily practice of visualizing your dreams as already complete can rapidly accelerate your achievement of those dreams, goals, and ambitions.

Step 1: Visualization of your goals and desires accomplishes four very important things.

1. It activates your creative subconscious (RAS) which will start generating creative ideas to achieve your goal.

2. It programs your brain to more readily perceive and recognize the resources you will need to achieve your dreams.

3. It activates the law of attraction, thereby drawing into your life the people, resources, and circumstances you will need to achieve your goals.

4. It builds your internal motivation to take the necessary actions to achieve your dreams.

Step 2: An important factor in accomplishing what matters most to you is committing your goals to writing. This is important for at least five reasons.

1. It will force you to clarify what you want.

2. It will motivate you to take action.

3. It will provide a filter for other opportunities.

4. It will help you overcome resistance.

5. It will enable you to see and celebrate your progress.

Writing your goals down is only the beginning. Articulating your intention is important, but it is not enough. You must execute your goals. You have to take action. I have found that writing down my goals and reviewing them regularly keeps me on track to completing my goals.

Step 3: Affirmations are positive statements about what you want. Repeating affirmations over and over helps you create what you want by imprinting your desires at both the conscious level and the subconscious level of your mind. To understand how this works, let's talk about how your conscious mind and your subconscious mind work.

Your conscious mind is where you do all of your thinking—it is the part of the mind that you are aware of. So when you say 2 + 2 = 4 you are using your conscious mind.

Your subconscious mind is the part of your brain that you are not aware of. It is like a giant filing cabinet that stores your memories, life experiences, belief systems and all the knowledge you have ever acquired in your entire life. And it has a much stronger influence on your thoughts, feelings, and behaviors than your conscious mind does.

The key to achieving your goals is to learn how to get your subconscious mind to work "for you" and not "against you." Positive affirmations are a great way to do this because your subconscious mind accepts as true what you tell it over and over again.

By intentionally and consciously using affirmations, you can "reprogram" your subconscious mind, which in turn can help you change your habits, your behavior, your attitude, and reshape your life!

Section One

Clarify and Set the Goal

I have a lot of success working with clients in various aspects of personal development such as goal achievement, health and wellness, spirituality and positive energy. One of the biggest obstacles standing in the way of their success is the failure to set clear goals and understand why they want to achieve the goals in the first place.

How can you know what you're shooting for if you cannot clearly visualize the goal you want to achieve? When you are working on goal achievement, setting and clarifying the goal is a necessary early step. So let's clarify and set your goals.

1. What are five things you would like to achieve?

2. Why do you want to achieve these particular goals?

3. What does accomplishing this mean to you?

4. **Now, go back to your list and prioritize.** If you could accomplish one of these right now, which one would it be? Why?

5. **Now that you have determined which one of these five is the most important area to work on right now, let's firm up this goal.** If you were vague when describing this goal, now is the time to get specific. For instance, if you wrote down lose weight, then write down how much weight you want to lose. Is it 20 pounds? 50? 100? If your goal is to start a new business, you should write down what you will accomplish in this new business.

6. **The next step to clarifying your goal is to put a time frame on it.** If you fail to attach a time frame to your goal, then that can make it difficult to evaluate your progress. The ability to evaluate your progress aids in keeping you motivated. Write down the time frame for achieving this goal. Also, write down why you have chosen this time frame. Remember it's "why" we do things that will help us persevere when times get tough.

7. **Now, go back and write out the complete goal, based on what you determined in this exercise.** Your goal should be specific and with a time frame. To carry on the weight loss example, your goal may be stated as: I will lose 20 pounds in three months.

Create the Plan

Doesn't it feel good to have a clearly defined goal? Knowing exactly what you want and why is a major step in the goal achievement process. You're no longer holding out a vague hope. You now have a clearly defined objective. This is one of the first things I have clients do when they come to me for personal development and goal achievement coaching.

Now that you know your goal and your time frame for achieving it, it's time to put together your plan. We've all heard the saying made famous by Benjamin Franklin, "If you fail to plan, you plan to fail." It's true. If you don't actually have a plan for achieving a thing, then there is a pretty good chance that thing won't happen!

Winging it isn't the approach you want to take here. Instead, you want to create a roadmap for your success. This will give you the actionable steps to take at each stage so you can progress along to completion. So, how do you work on achieving a goal when you don't know what goes into it?

Well, you've got to educate yourself about it. A common mistake that people make is thinking that their roadmap has to be something that is original to them. It is wiser to try to learn what successful people have done before you. By studying other successful people, younot only learn from their successes, but you also have the opportunity to learn from their mistakes.

The first assignment in creating your plan for successfully completing your goal is to become knowledgeable about it.

1. **Learn from those who have already done it.** Who are five people you admire who have achieved this thing you are attempting? Write down their names, as well as briefly describe what they have achieved, relative to this particular area. For instance, if your goal is to raise $20,000 to feed hungry children in your community, then write down the names of others who have conducted successful fundraisers, and (briefly) write down what they accomplished. For instance, you might write down that Joe Smith raised $100,000 for relief after the 2010 Haiti earthquake.

2. **Study the approach and methods of the successful.** Now, research what each of these five people did to accomplish their goal. Your research may include an Internet search of each person and their accomplishment, reading biographies of these people, visiting their websites and reading material they have produced, or seeing if any of these people have posted YouTube videos. Write down the highlights of your research here. Use additional paper, if necessary.

3. **What are the commonalities among all?** Are there several things you see that keep coming up with these people you have studied? If so, note those things here. For instance, using the fundraising example, you might have noticed they all started with their inner circles and asked for donations and support from them. Or you might find that they all used crowdfunding. Whatever commonality you see, write about it here.

Now, research the topic related to your goal. For instance, using the example of raising money to feed children in your community, you might do a search on "best ways to raise money for charity." Read as many articles as you can. Audiobooks are also a powerful tool to have at your disposal. You'll begin to see some suggestions and ideas repeated several times. You'll also come across best practices and other necessary information. All of this will help educate you about the steps necessary to achieving your goal.

4. **Based on your research of people who have been successful in this area, as well as your research on the topic itself, write down as many steps to accomplishing your goal as you can identify.**

5. **Write down the resources you will need for accomplishing this goal.** These may be resources you identified through your research of the steps, or resources you realize you will need after completing Exercise 4 in this section. For instance, you may realize you will need a certain type of equipment, or a certain amount of money, or even to learn a new skill. Include any and all resources you will need to accomplish this goal.

6. **Now, create your plan.** Based on the approach and the resources you've identified, put together a step-by-step plan for achieving your goal. Start with Step 1 and go all the way through as many steps as necessary. Write out your multi-step plan here:

You've made a lot of progress on creating your plan, but you've still got one critical part to do. You must put some dates to those actions! Setting aside appropriate time to dedicate to working on your goal is extremely important. If you don't set aside—and actually schedule—the time, achievement of your goal probably won't happen. That's because the demands of life will likely crowd out your plans. If you don't clear the time to make your plans a reality, you'll keep putting your action steps off for another day.

So, attach a date to each step. Using your smartphone, tablet, computer calendar, or a printed calendar, schedule each step on a specific date in your calendar.

Congratulations! Your plan is in place. Now, it's time to work it.

Work the Plan

When working your goal achievement plan, it can be tempting to put off the less desirable tasks. Every success has some tasks attached to it that are not as fun, as glamorous or as interesting as others. But handling those tasks right alongside the fun, glamorous and interesting tasks is just as important—maybe even more important, in some instances.

So, this part of the workbook is dedicated to helping you work on your goal achievement plan specifically.

1. **What are the daily tasks you must do to keep progressing toward your goal?** Review your plan and write out those tasks that must be done daily or frequently.

2. **What are the toughest tasks you will face in executing your plan?** Write down which tasks you dread tackling or are simply not excited about doing.

The reason it's important to identify the tasks that you aren't as interested in doing is that you need to be aware of what you're facing, so you know how to overcome it. Going back to the fundraising example, if you dread making calls to potential donors, then you may keep putting this task off, never quite getting around to it.

In doing so, you may sabotage your own fundraising efforts and never accomplish your goal. So, don't be so afraid of doing things you least like to do. Be honest. Take the time to identify which tasks in your plan may cause you a bit of trouble.

3. **What can I do to overcome this problem?** Now that you have identified the tasks that may be problematic for you, write down at least two ways you can address and overcome each of these difficulties.

For instance, if your goal is to lose weight, but you hate going to the gym, write down how you can get beyond this. You might write down that you will go for runs through the neighborhood instead of the gym, or that you can install a home gym, or that you will go through a fitness boot camp put on by a local personal trainer at an area park.

If you would like more examples of how to overcome obstacles while creating your action plan you can contact me directly at **www. reverseeffect.com.**

Addressing the barriers to your progress helps set you up for success. In this section, you have not only identified the parts of your plan that may cause you stress or cause you to give up on your plan, but you have come up with solutions to those problems. This will help you to keep moving forward!

Section Four

Deal with Setbacks

No matter how well we plan, we're sure to run into some setbacks on the way to accomplishing our goals and living out our dreams. That's why I've included this section in this workbook.

It would be easy to think that the steps you've already completed in this workbook will set you on easy street when it comes to goal achievement. But they won't. Following all of these steps will make goal achievement a lot easier and definitely more likely, but no plan can prevent all setbacks.

That's why you've got to be ready for them. You see, even if you plan perfectly, sometimes unforeseen challenges arise. That is called life. In *The Reverse Effect*, I talk about the benefits of having a proactive mindset as opposed to a reactive mindset. This helps you overcome unexpected challenges. When you have a reactive mindset, you are just going with the flow of things instead of taking charge and directing the flow in the direction that you wish. When you have a reactive mindset, you will always seem to be caught off guard by life's ups and downs.

By contrast, when you have a proactive mindset you tend to solve matters before they become an issue. People with the proactive mindset have a significant advantage over most people in life. They are flexible and adapt well to the continual changes that life throws at them.

Have you ever been doing great with a goal or habit change—exercise, waking early, becoming organized, eating healthy, anything—and your progress was completely disrupted because of some major event in your life like death, marriage, illness, work, etc.? Of course, you have. It's happened to all of us!

Fortunately, although we often give up on our goals when something like this happens, a life event that disrupts your progress doesn't have to sidetrack your goal completely. You can overcome this obstacle!

That's why this section is here. It's your "What to do in case life happens" section.

1. **Plan for the unexpected.** To the extent you can, have a contingency plan. For example, using the weight loss example, you may suffer an injury that prevents you from running but doesn't affect swimming. So, maybe you switch your cardio to swimming instead of running. Though you may be using a different method, you can still accomplish your goal.

Write down as many "worst-case" scenarios as you can think of when pursuing your goal. As with previous exercises, use additional paper, if necessary.

2. **An obstacle is just something we have to get around or over... it's not a reason to quit.** So, instead of quitting, ask yourself: How do I get around this obstacle? There's always a solution if you're resourceful enough. In this next exercise, let's be very creative and utilize all the resources at your disposal to solve potential setbacks.

Use methods such as researching other people who have accomplished the same goal that you are accomplishing and see how they overcame obstacles that were set in their paths. Also, draw on your own experiences of dealing with obstacles.

Now, for each such scenario, write down any adjustments you can make when obstacles come up on your path to achieving a goal.

Just as in the previous section, writing down ways to address a potential problem can be extremely beneficial. Here, writing down potential setbacks and how you can address them will help you feel empowered in the event the worst does happen. It also can help keep your spirits up, so you don't get too disappointed or discouraged in the midst of the setback because you realize there is something you can do.

You will face some setbacks every now and then. That's a part of achieving any goal worth achieving—if it's too easy, it's not a worthy goal. But instead of seeing the setback as something discouraging, just accept it as a part of the journey. Learn how to make adjustments and keep pushing forward.

This is part of having a growth mindset: not allowing a setback to define who you are, but instead seeing it as a source of information. Make it a point to remind yourself of the progress that you have made. You know the adage, "Two steps forward, one step back." When you come to the realization that even with setbacks, you're still making forward progress over the long run—that's **The Reverse Effect**.

If you would like one-on-one help to deal with obstacles while you are on the path of completing your goals, contact me at **www.clintonmmccoy.com**

Accomplish the Goal

Ah, success! Success is an amazing feeling. It's what we work toward when we do set out to achieve a certain goal. As you work diligently and purposefully on the tasks of accomplishing your goals, I also want to help you work on your mind. Having a positive mindset is vital to accomplishing the goals.

If you fall, get up and learn from it.

All of us fail from time to time. No one is successful all the time. But instead of letting failure stop you completely, you just need to get up and dust yourself off… and this part is important: Learn from your experience. When you fail, ask yourself: Why did I fail? What stopped me? What obstacles got in my way? And how can I get around them the next time it happens? And how can I get around them the next time it happens? And yes, it will happen again. Plan for the next time.

I have found that the mind is actually the most important part of goal achievement. Everything we want happens first in the mind. In fact, we create our own realities, starting with our minds. So get your mind right! Prepare to be transformed into a goal achievement machine!

The Bible says in Romans 12:2 (KJV), "Be ye transformed by the renewing of your mind."

How that applies here is that when you work on your mind, when you come to a new way of thinking, then you can transform your life. The old ways of thinking created the old habits that have sought to trap you in your current reality. You are ready for a new reality, one of achieving goals and creating success!

One way to renew your mind and create transformation in your thinking is by engaging in creative visualization. Creative visualization is the act of visualizing what you want to happen, rather than focusing on what you don't want to happen.

It's about actually capturing and holding onto a positive vision of your goal. It's about seeing yourself accomplish the thing before it actually happens in real life. For more about creative visualization, see Chapter 18 "Keys for Success" in *The Reverse Effect*.

Creative visualization helps program you for success. It allows you to see yourself as empowered, successful and accomplishing your dreams. It gives you just the boost you need to keep going and actually accomplish your goals.

1. **Set the scene for your success.** Close your eyes and visualize what your life would be like if you were to accomplish the goals you've outlined for yourself. Then open your eyes and write about it here. Use all of your senses to describe this reality.

2. **Now, hold onto this vision.** Write it down in a place where you can carry and see it every day. This can be a 3 x 5 note card, or it can be saved to your smartphone. Make a practice of reflecting on this vision daily. Reflect on it on days when everything is going along well, so the vision can sustain you when things aren't going quite as well. On those days when you don't quite feel like doing the tasks contained in your plan, or when a setback has occurred, pull out this vision and wrap yourself in it again.

When you commit to a thing—such as achieving a certain goal—and you are earnest in your intention, then creative visualization is one tool that can help to alert your reticular activating system.

Your reticular activating system (RAS) is housed at the base of your brain and acts as your filtering system. Your brain receives thousands of messages every second, and you simply could not function if every one of those messages came to your conscious mind.

So, your reticular activating system protects you by only allowing certain information to get through to your conscious mind. What happens in the context of goal achievement is that when you commit to doing a thing, and you are seeking information about it, your reticular activating system then works to bring information about it to your attention. So, if you are pursuing the goal you've just identified in this workbook, and you are working diligently on making it happen, then your reticular activating system (the brain's filter) looks for information to bring to your conscious mind.

An example of how the reticular activating system works can be found in a common decision like buying a new shirt. Have you ever bought a shirt, then suddenly started noticing all the other people wearing that same type of shirt?

If so, then that was your reticular activating system in action. Where you may not have noticed this shirt being worn by others before, your reticular activating system now brings this information to your awareness.

How this helps with goal achievement is that you will start to notice information, resources, and opportunities related to your goal. That information and those resources and opportunities may have been around all along, but because they weren't important to you at that time, you didn't notice them.

But now, by committing to your goal and doing the exercises in this workbook, you now notice them, thanks to your reticular activating system.

3. **Keep pressing forward towards achieving your goal.** Let your reticular activating system bring to your awareness the information that can assist you on your journey. Follow the steps to your plan. Hold on to that vision by reflecting on it each day. Be flexible and make adjustments as necessary so that a setback doesn't become a permanent stop. Do this, and you will achieve your goal! I know because this has helped me, and it's helped others I've worked with. I know this can help you, too.

REFERENCES

Blaslotto, Judd Dr., University of Michigan.

Dweck, Carol Dr., (2016). *Mindset: The Psychology of Success*. New York: Ballantine Books.

Dyer, Wayne Dr., Author and Motivational Speaker.

Holland, Ron G. (2012). *Turbo Success*.

Holy Bible (KJV and NKJV).

Kübler-Ross, Elisabeth Dr., Swiss American Psychiatrist.

Maltz, Maxwell M.D. (2002), *The New Psycho*.

Maslow, Abraham Dr., Psychologist.

McCain, John, United States Senator, Arizona.

Obama, Barack H., 44th President of the United States.

Robbins, Anthony, Motivational Speaker.

Tzu, Lao (1954). *Tao Te Ching*.

Tzu, Sun. Chinese Military General, Strategist, Philosopher (4th-5th Century).

Xi, Zhu, Song Dynasty Scholar (12th Century).

Yang Ming, Wang. Chinese Neo-Confucian Philosopher (15th Century). *The Unity of Knowledge and Action*.

ABOUT THE AUTHOR

Clinton M. McCoy is a personal development and goal achievement expert with a passion for helping people unlock their potential. Drawing from personal and academic experience, Clinton has transformed his life on the personal, professional and spiritual levels. Through the years, Clinton has worked tirelessly on developing the tools that he has used in his transformation into a format that could be spread to others. Through these efforts was born *"The Reverse Effect."*

The Reverse Effect focuses on what he names The Four Quadrants of Well-Being. Each quadrant represents a cornerstone of overall success and personal fulfillment. These quadrants are personal and relationship development, goal achievement, and health and wellness. His passion is to teach a masterful balance between these four quadrants that will help you unlock your potential and become the master of your circumstances.

Today, Clinton is an accomplished Life Coach, Personal Fitness Trainer, Mentor, and Successful Businessman. He believes in giving back to the community through building his Chess 4 Change Program designed to help at-risk youth learn how to set goals and achieve them. He lives his life as proof that you can create the life you want!

> *"Life is 10% of what happens to you and*
> *90% how you react to it!"*
> *~ Clinton M. McCoy*

Great, you finish the book, but now what? The journey begins. I know I can help you get to your desired destination faster so let's stay connected. I share LOTS of content on Facebook, Instagram, LinkedIn and YouTube. Whichever platform you choose to follow me at (and I would not mind if you followed me in all ☺) you will gain the clarity, confidence and momentum you need to go from potential to peak performance.

Also, don't forget to grab your FREE planner here: bit.ly/thereverseeffectplanner

Remember, you ALREADY possess everything you need to transform your life.

Clinton

My Social Media Platforms

Facebook: https://www.facebook.com/clinton.m.mccoy/
Facebook Community: https://www.facebook.com/groups/passionpurposetoprosperity/
Instagram: https://www.instagram.com/clinton_m_mccoy/
YouTube: http://bit.ly/clintonmccoyyoutube
LinkedIn: https://www.linkedin.com/in/clinton-m-mccoy/
My Website: https://www.clintonmmccoy.com/

NOTES

NOTES

NOTES

NOTES

Made in the USA
Columbia, SC
18 June 2023